Single...
Not by Choice

*Emotional and Financial Guidance for
Women After the Loss of Their Spouse*

*From the Authors of
The Sudden Wealth Book Series*

DAVID RUST and SHANE MOORE

Copyright © 2018 The Sudden Wealth Center™

All rights reserved.
ISBN: 1983984337
ISBN-13: 978-1983984334

DISCLAIMERS

This publication is intended to be an informative and narrative piece outlining key areas of wealth management, specifically related to sudden windfalls. It is not intended to be prescriptive or to imply endorsement of the products, strategies, or processes discussed in the following stories or supporting text.

This publication is designed to provide accurate and authoritative information with the understanding that the publisher is not engaged in rendering legal, accounting, or other professional services. If legal advice or other expert assistance is required, the services of a competent professional should be sought.

DEDICATION

This book is dedicated to all the strong, brave women we are fortunate to know. It is also dedicated to the men they shared their lives with that are no longer with us. We wish emotional and financial health to all the widows who daily face and meet the challenges of being *Single... Not by Choice*.

CONTENTS

Acknowledgments 1

Preface 5

Introduction 9

Chapter 1: Alone 15

Chapter 2: Seven Words 27

Chapter 3: Now What? 39

Chapter 4: Living Without Him 57

Chapter 5: Your *New* Normal 69

Chapter 6: Defining Your Goals 83

Chapter 7: Reflections 105

Chapter 8: Resources 113

    Is it Time to See a Therapist? 115

The Wealth Wheel 119
Duties of the Executor 139
Building Your Team 161
Financial Discovery 173
Preparing for Your Estate Planning Review 185
Preparing for Your Property Insurance Review 191

Chapter 9: Memories 197

Epilogue 227

About the Authors 231

ACKNOWLEDGMENTS

In the creation of our first book, *Sudden Wealth... It Happens*, one of our clients mentioned that "Rust and Moore never sleep." If you knew us well, you would know there is some truth to that statement! During the creation of this book, there were some sleepless times. Most of the sleeplessness was due to the tremendous responsibility we felt to the widows we interviewed. They were the impetus to complete *Single... Not by Choice*. The widows that we know, the widows that allowed us to interview them, the widows we read about, and the millions of widows around the world. While we still can't fathom the extent of your grief, we are so thankful to you for sharing your stories. Your honesty and your ability to share your difficult journey allowed us to write this book so, thank you.

We thank the professional alliances we have as estate planning attorneys, CPA's, bankers, property and casualty specialists, real estate professionals and trust administrators. We can't truly handle the comprehensive needs of widows without you. We thank you for sharing the vision of comprehensive care for our clients.

Another critical alliance is with our psychiatrists, psychotherapists, and family therapists. They continue to be a vital resource both to us and to some of our clients, friends, and family. In writing this book, they were always willing to share their expertise and experience with us. We thank them for what they mean to us, and our firm. They continue to teach us that while the numbers are an important element of our job as financial advisors, we must always be aware of the personal and emotional challenges our clients may be experiencing, particularly in the case of widows.

Acknowledgments

We are grateful to those of you who shared your favorite memories of your husbands and fathers. We honor their lives by keeping their memories top of mind.

We thank Brian Talbot, the "Voice of Quartz" in our Sudden Wealth Videos and our Marketing Guru, for reminding us that we have a responsibility to convey the challenges of all types of sudden wealth. His conclusion that the time to write the book on widows is now, and his encouragement to finish was instrumental in writing this book.

We thank Brad Closson, our Business Coach for convincing us to write our very first book 7 years ago, and for being a calm voice of reason when we think we may have bitten off more than we could chew. Brad is a great advisor and friend.

We thank Lori Dumas for being one of our trusted editors and allowing us to bounce ideas off her. We thank her for the strong presence she is every day for our clients.

Our wives Cyndee Rust and Carol Moore never blink when we tell them about the next big thing we want to do. Their continual encouragement and belief in us is a tremendous motivator when things get tough. We can't thank them enough for their support of Quartz, *The Sudden Wealth Book Series*, and *The Sudden Wealth Video Series*.

And finally, we thank our clients for allowing us to work with them on the many different services that comprise our Family Office Services. Our clients are great people and we are honored to work for them. We wish them continued financial and emotional health.

PREFACE

In the Preface of our second book, *Sudden Wealth… Blessing or Burden*, we posed the question to our readers, "What do we know about Sudden Wealth now that we didn't know when we wrote our first book?" The answer, "quite a lot actually," was just as true then as it is today. After writing 3 books and speaking around the country to both consumers and financial advisors who work for them, we wondered what else could we learn and what else could we share? As "numbers guys," our research lead us down the obvious path. With the average life expectancy of men at around 83 years and women some two to three years later, it's clear that more women will experience the loss of their spouse than vice versa. Specializing in sudden wealth, we have helped more than a few widows over our careers maneuver through the financial challenges when the person primarily responsible for the finances passes either suddenly or after a lengthy illness. While we guide them toward a strategic path financially and offer support on the emotional side through our professional partnerships of talented therapists, we wondered, "Were we missing something?"

We discovered in writing this book that we had much to learn to fully understand the depths of emotions when a wife loses her husband. We suspect that there are many people who also lack that understanding. Luckily the many strong and unique women we interviewed as part of this process were more than willing to share their stories and wisdom with us. Our goal was to write a book worthy enough for other women to read, gain comfort and sound guidance. We want this book to be a guiding light during the most difficult period in their lives. We also want to share this book with anyone who knows or loves a widow. A guide to help people understand the widow's pain, to know what to say to them and what not to say, to understand that their grief ebbs and flows, diminishes over time, but never truly goes away.

We heard more than a few times that two men writing a book about women and the deaths of their husbands is maybe not well thought out. We were told that we should consider having a woman co-author. After all, how can two guys possibly understand this extremely personal situation and give advice about it? Initially they were perhaps smart to question us. But something amazing happened along the way. We spoke with widows and daughters of widows and therapists and attorneys of widows. **We learned to ask better questions.** We became better listeners. Each story, each "aha moment" for us made us more committed than ever to create a valuable tool for all widows and for those who love or care about them.

Yes, we are financial advisors and we understand our primary role. But we believe to be the BEST advisors we can be, we needed to better understand the magnitude of the situation from the side of our client. After countless hours of conversations, and research, we now know that we can't fully understand their loss, their grief, their fear of their new future, the unknown. While we patiently walk them down the important and necessary financial steps, we'll do so with an enhanced appreciation of their current burden and daily challenges along with their future concerns.

Thank you for reading our book. If any part of it speaks to you, changes your life or habits, please let us know. We would be happy to hear from you.

INTRODUCTION

Our journey writing the *Sudden Wealth Book Series* has been enlightening, to say the least. As wealth advisors specializing in these life events, we believe it is impossible to do our best job without understanding the nuances of the emotional aspects associated with the situation that created the wealth. Years of advising clients in these situations have proved to be both exciting and thought-provoking.

Whether a loss of a spouse, business sale, retirement, lottery, or divorce creates sudden wealth, the emotional components of each can cause a tremendous ripple in the fabric of each family. That is why it is critical for us to ask deeper questions and address these real-life issues in conjunction with the typical wealth planning strategies and techniques.

We have personally witnessed the initial fear that sudden wealth typically creates. The fear of the unknown, the fear of making a mistake, the fear that leaves some unable to make necessary decisions, are all too common. By understanding this fear, we can have a better understanding of how to explain each step and to adjust the pace of necessary topics to address.

These fears and other emotional challenges lead us to write a book about widows. There is most likely no greater traumatic event than the loss of a spouse. While we have worked with widows for years, we wanted to know more about how women are specifically feeling and reacting emotionally to this trauma.

In our research, we interviewed widows, daughters of widows, therapists, and estate planning attorneys of widows. Some of them lost their husbands through a lengthy illness and some from a sudden death. The women we spoke with ranged from the early thirties to the early eighties. Some had lost their husbands many years ago and some merely months before. The therapists we spoke with were instrumental in providing additional information and guidance on interview questions. Their attorneys shared their best cases and worst nightmares.

In our practice, our primary work consists of providing guidance for the financial steps that are necessary after the death of a spouse. We then develop a plan and execute that plan in tandem with the widow's goals and objectives. This book provides an extensive amount of information, steps, and suggestions for a widow to follow. It can serve as an excellent guide for any person as well. Along with these financial and legal resources, we hope to convey through the voices of each woman we interviewed, the trauma, the challenges, and the hopes and healing that each shared with us.

This book is written for any person who has lost their spouse or is a family member, friend or advisor of someone who has lost their spouse. Our hope is that every widow who reads it will gain insight and comfort from hearing from others who have already walked in their shoes. Our hope is that it gives them strength by knowing that others like them have eventually walked "out of the fog." Our hope is that this book can serve as a guidepost to all of us to know how to act, what to say and to be more empathetic with any woman who is currently engaged in this traumatic event whether it is has been weeks since their husband's death or years.

The book is written in the order of a widow's journey. It starts off explaining the intense feelings of being lonely and the day to day challenges of being alone. Chapter 2 walks the reader through the weeks and months prior to death if there was a lengthy illness, including the shock of getting the news of a sudden death. We then walk the reader through the immediate days and months after his death. The ensuing chapters will delve into the emotional and financial challenges she faces. We provide specific guidelines/resources for the financial and legal hurdles as the weeks, months and years go by. Throughout the book, we convey the challenges and feelings they deal with on the emotional side. The later chapters talk about her new normal and how to deal with the subsiding but ever-present grief.

Some of this book is difficult to read. For us, some of their stories were difficult to hear. Can you imagine how hard it is for the widows? We truly hope we have clearly conveyed the challenges of the journey they face. We hope that the insight gained by reading this book will help you understand and be more patient and empathetic of the widow's journey.

ALONE

"Don't go away. I don't want to be alone. I can't stand being alone."

Arnold Rothstein

It's interesting that as I sit at my computer to write this chapter, it is quiet in the house and the feeling of being alone is glaringly present. Writing can be a lonely activity. Writing a chapter on loneliness is especially difficult to write. And while after months of research, I may now have a better idea of the magnitude of the aloneness a widow feels, I'm sure my understanding barely touches

Single... Not by Choice

their feeling of isolation.

The latest statistics on the number of widows in the United States is staggering. **There are over 13 million widows in the U.S. and approximately 700,000 lose their husbands each year.** The United Nations (AP) reported in 2010 that at least 245 million women around the world have been widowed. The countries with the highest number of widows were China with 43 million, India with 42 million, the United States with 13.6 million, Indonesia with 9.4 million, Japan with 7.4 million, Russia with 7.1 million and several other countries with over 4 million widows. Of all married women, 75% will be widowed at least once in their lives. Despite common beliefs that becoming a widow is the sentence of older women, the average age of a woman in the United States who will lose her husband is 55 and 33% will lose her spouse before age 45.

As a widow, would hearing these numbers make you feel "less alone"? After all, you are one of the millions around the world going through the very same event. As part of life's natural journey, would hearing these numbers help you prepare for the statistically inevitable? As a loved one, would these numbers give you the idea that this experience is somehow very common? Our interviews showed us that nothing can prepare them for this tragedy and as statistically likely as it may be, no one is ever ready for it.

Each woman we interviewed wanted to make sure we knew their journey was different than the rest. We assured each of them that their journey being different was a certainty. However, all of them mentioned two similar feelings "overwhelmed" and "alone." We understand these feelings may be unfamiliar to them, in fact, it is our job to set the pace, so they feel "less overwhelmed," at least with the financial aspects of their new present and future. The word "alone" is understandable as they have lost their person, their way of life, their confidant, their history and their future (all descriptions we heard from them). We have tried to understand the magnitude of being alone and how it affects their decision making especially when it comes to their own financial health and how it affects their physical and emotional health. As their advisors and friends, understanding their aloneness is hard, but we wanted to know more and perhaps come to terms with a better way to help them.

The feeling of being alone makes all the sense in the world when you consider that many of these women were with their spouse over 25 years, some over 50 years. Many of them met as teenagers and were tied together through history as friends, partners, spouses, parents, and grandparents. The days and experiences that bind them are part of the fabric of their being as they shared the good times and the bad times.

They told us after their spouse died, that there was a "hole in them," that truly a part of them was now missing and no amount of support from family or friends could fill that hole. They say that their life during these early weeks and months was a complete "blur." A few said they experienced "grief brain" and at times needed to be reminded to eat, to pay bills, not to mention to sleep. They said that nighttime is the worst. At night, their loneliness is extreme and the anxiety that often accompanies it only exacerbates the loneliness experienced by their new reality – one bed, one person. This is when they feel most alone and are left with their own mind, spirit, and faith to cope until the night ends and the sun rises their loneliness continues like the same song with a different tune.

What about the widows who lost their husbands suddenly or after being married for a relatively short time? Is their loneliness different? We were told that the "what ifs" are significant and their loneliness can focus on the future that they always dreamed of but was suddenly cut way too short. Their level of shock is magnified. Many times, they didn't get to say goodbye. They weren't prepared, why should they be? Their brains ruminate over the children they never had or the future their children will now have with only one parent. They feel guilty because the last time they spoke to him was an argument or disagreement. They are angry at him for abandoning them and that worsens the guilt they feel. They talked about the stress they feel over handling all parenting responsibilities instead of sharing the duties with their life partner. In many situations, their lives together were just getting started, now what?

While those of us who support widows as family members or friends are in constant motion to help them feel less lonely, it is a fact that the journey they now walk is clearly their own. Just the number of things they now do by themselves is a constant reminder of their new status—single, widowed, alone. One of the widows interviewed talked about the challenge of taking her young son to birthday parties. She cringed every time she got a birthday invitation for him. When we asked why, she told us that since her son's father died when her son was a year old, the barrage of questions about the whereabouts of her husband or the questions to her son, such as "Where's your daddy?" would inevitably come from mom's and children. On every occasion, she had to explain her situation. It made her feel as though she was continually reliving the entire memory. This continued especially when her son changed school's years later and to this day as her son turns 10.

We often see in our practice where the husband paid all the bills, handled the investments and any financial and legal responsibilities. Now tackling these duties without him leaves many of them feeling helpless, anxiety-ridden, and paralyzed. The fear of being the sole decision maker magnifies how alone they feel. While we do everything we can to direct them to a calm and easy pace, without walking in their shoes it is tough to truly understand just how difficult it is for them. Before doing this research, we would slow the pace of necessary financial steps, but rarely if ever mentioned the deceased. We were told that this made them feel more alone. That was a huge lesson for us to learn. It is a lesson, we're sure many of us could learn.

Even activities like going to church by themselves can be a stress-inducing event. While fellow worshipers and church friends mean well, **we were told that the number of questions from well-intentioned people can become so overwhelming that they would rather just not attend in some cases.** Imagine a faith-filled person so consumed with being alone, that the sheer thought of going to church freezes them with fear and anxiety.

As part of a couple, they shared the lives of their other married friends through vacations, card games, concerts and wine tastings and other events. These events can become awkward invitations now, as they feel like the odd person out or in some cases, she becomes persona non-grata for fear that she may be looked at differently by the husbands. In many cases, the wives of her couples' friends now see her as a threat to their own marriages. As hard as that is to believe, we heard that situation more than once. Either way, these events that were historically perfect for the two of them, become a continual reminder that he's no longer there and the loneliness strikes a familiar chord.

Listening to their stories and understanding the magnitude of how alone they feel, gives us information and in fact makes us feel the need to take action on their behalf. **We** think we can get them through this. **We**, meaning their family, their friends. In fact, there are many additional resources available for them from their church, professional support groups to therapists and blogs. We believe that the therapists we know and work with can play a tremendous role in helping them with their grief, but a widow must raise her hand and choose to do it. It is up to them to choose to utilize any of the resources available to them. Some of them find relief in these resources while others can't muster the energy or accept the need for help in spite of the fact that they are going through one of life's most devastating events according to the Holmes and Rahe Stress Scale.

No one should have to go through one of life's most devastating events alone. Yet despite the love, support, good intentions of family and friends, they actually do walk the journey alone. As devastating and traumatic as it may be, the path is wide enough for only one. It can be excruciating for their loved ones to watch this journey, so it begs the question, "Can we allow them to be alone in their pain?" or must we try to "fix it"?

Our research revealed that many family members, friends, and advisors are particularly uncomfortable handling the challenges of a grieving loved one, friend or client. At times it forces us to look at ourselves and our own feelings of losing someone close to us. Some of us just don't handle it well and because of this can end up adding additional challenges to the bereaved. This was reiterated in many of our interviews as they spoke specifically about how hard it is trying to be strong for everyone else.

Single... Not by Choice

We were told that one of the best ways to help someone during their grief is to be specific in the help you would like to give. Instead of saying, "Is there anything I can do for you?", be specific with suggestions such as "I'd like to bring lunch to you on Thursday."; "I would like to make a salad and spaghetti with meat sauce. Is that something that sounds good to you?"; or, "Will you go see a movie with me this week? " I'm thinking Friday early and I can come pick you up." Those are just a few examples of ways they said being specific matters so much to them. They told us that even having to make the easiest decisions was exhausting.

So, we've confirmed that the death of a spouse is one of life's most devastating events. It begins a journey that few are prepared for and it is a journey that must be walked alone. While they have support and resources, sometimes the support of loved ones and friends can fall short. As loved ones and friends of the bereaved, it can bring up issues inside each of us, that make it more difficult to help them handle the stress. We can't fix them. We can't eliminate the tremendous pain they feel every day.

We read a speech recently that summed this up.

Alone

The speech was given by Dr. Christopher B. Teel at a high school induction ceremony at Emery High School. His general thesis was about the scripts of our lives, understanding and honoring the unknown. **He posed the question, "Are we alone?"** Our own communities aside, he said,

> "We are alone in our responsibilities to ourselves. We are responsible for responding to everything that happens to us. Some of it will be great, some of it will suck. But it's all on us. There's no one else to blame for our misery, our joy, our challenges, our choices, our complexities. It's on us to create meaning in our lives. So, we've got to honor that responsibility. That responsibility to ourselves. We've got to honor being alone in that way."

Perhaps, in some way a widow owes a responsibility not only to herself but to her husband and the union they shared to find a way every day to continue breathing, never forgetting his memory, and finding the next chapter in her life. As for her loved ones and friends and yes even her advisors, perhaps we should trust that she will find her way down a long road, on her own.

SEVEN WORDS

"The deeper that sorrow carves into your being, the more joy you can contain."

Khalil Gibran

The women who shared their nightmare with us said that it often starts with seven words, "I'm afraid I have some bad news." Seven words and the clock starts on a journey that can last from days to weeks to years. Seven words begin the biggest change in their life. Seven words pierce their hearts, hit them in the gut, sucks the air right out of their lungs. They become overwhelmed with sadness, fear, anxiety, anger all at once. The range of emotions is so wide that many told us it was just simply too hard for them to grasp.

Most were offered hope and encouragement along with those seven words. Others expressed frustration and anger with how this information was delivered, perhaps that the doctor spoke with little feeling and offered little consolation or hope. With tears in her eyes, she shrugged it off as an inexperienced doctor. If hearing that their husband had suddenly died, disbelief and shock covered all the words by a described fog that we heard about from every single widow we interviewed.

Whether a lengthy illness leading to death or a sudden death, these women began carrying the load as wife, mother, caregiver and many, if not all of the duties, that normally were taken care of by their husband for years. The mental and physical toll on them is tremendous. They are often pushed to the brink.

For those women whose husbands were ill and experienced a long journey with doctors and hospitals before they passed, they may have felt deep anger and resentment for the changes in responsibilities, their long journey as a caretaker, and the fact that the scale tipped for a very long time. Their grieving may have started months before their husband's death. They miss their partner, their protector, their best friend, as they hold his hand in a hospital room. They may feel unappreciated by their husband during this time. The illness may not allow him to show his appreciation at all. We heard that they could feel the unspeakable and a great amount of guilt for sometimes wishing that the inevitable end come sooner and at the same time wondering how they will survive without him. They may feel uncertain because he handled the finances and things like the yard work or car care. The realization that she doesn't know all his passwords, seemingly not the most important thing, may come up at an inopportune time.

In the instance of a sudden death, the magnitude of the shock is indescribable. The words in that case usually come from a stranger, perhaps a policeman or a Military Chaplain. The unimaginable is the woman that discovers her husband from a suicide. A normal day turns on a dime when the news is delivered. The news makes time stop for this woman and at the same time, there are so many things that will need to happen quickly. The flurry of activity around her baffles the mind. At the same time, she may be wondering if he suffered much. She didn't get to say goodbye and sometimes her last words may not have been pleasant and guilt surfaces. In most cases, family and friends immediately rally around her. Unlike a lengthy illness, she had no time to prepare and many times pre-funeral arrangements weren't made. Meeting with the funeral home and making decisions on caskets and funeral plans and writing an obituary need to be done immediately. Imagine yourself in this chaos.

Whether the death was sudden or after a lengthy illness, it starts a fog that slaps a widow in the face and envelopes them as the day and weeks go by. This "fog" has often been mentioned to describe the moment of the death and subsequent time where they also describe themselves as "going through the motions." Many said they don't know how they got through the funeral. Several were medicated during the initial days of the death to help them with anxiety and uncontrollable emotions. Each remembers speaking to every person who attended the funeral yet describes the process as a "sea of faces." They leaned on their family and close friends and were rarely if ever disappointed by the level of support they received. Nights were typically the worst. In many cases, they would have friends or family members spend the night. This may go on for days or even weeks. The fog prevents them from eating, from focusing. The fog makes them tell you with an immediate response, "I'm fine." when you ask them how they are doing. Apparently, that is THE question they hear more than any. This fog years later makes it hard for them to describe the period from their husband's death to months and sometimes years later. The fog prevents them from finding the words to your question no matter how simple the question may be.

As disorienting as this fog may seem to those around them, it may be that the fog could be protecting a widow from a pain so extreme that for some time, it prevents them from feeling the pain they are in. It can be a powerful coping mechanism, although during our interviews the fog made it difficult to understand what they were feeling during this time as their memories and details are cloudy and vague.

Fear of the unknown and fear of facing odds stacked against them can create severe anxiety on top of everything else they are facing. In many cases, anti-anxiety drugs were prescribed and to get through the funeral to a few days after. As part of our education for this book, we interviewed therapists and psychiatrists who told us to look for serious signs of depression. Some of these signs include loss of appetite, inability to sleep or concentrate, a loss of self-esteem, and mentioning they have nothing to live for, as a few of the signs. It helps anyone close to them to know if they are functioning at basic levels like bathing and buying groceries or taking care of their pets. These are markers that may indicate the need to see a psychiatrist for prescription medication, supervision, and a form of therapy.

Death of a spouse is the #1 stressor according to the Homes and Rahe Stress Scale[i] and there can be a snowball effect that can occur as a result of the loss. **60% of those who lose a spouse or significant other will experience a serious**

illness in the 12 months that follow that loss. Serious illness may be prevented by taking care of themselves and by family members making sure that her care is of primary importance during this time. And a big key to taking care of herself is also one of her biggest challenges – sleeping. When it is quiet at night, the mind begins to wonder, fear and anxiety begin to rise. The empty side of the bed becomes the nightly reminder that he's no longer there to talk to anymore. Hearing their husband's voice when in acute grief is common but confusing to them as it seems so real. Not sleeping continues to be an ongoing problem in acute grief. When not sleeping becomes chronic, sleep medication may be necessary for an extended period.

In Chapter 1 we spoke of the feeling of being alone. It is rare to hear any widow not talk about the tremendous support they received from family and friends. However, we have also heard widows say that while many were there for them, they just "didn't get it." That sentiment backs our thesis on being alone, that while surrounded by loves ones, they still feel very isolated. While family and friends remain empathetic especially during, the early days and weeks after the death, how could they "get it" unless they have personally experienced it? And even if they have experienced it we believe that every woman believes in her heart that her specific situation is completely different from all the other widows who have walked the same walk. This is an important component of the acute grief phase and a big takeaway for us as financial advisors. **We can be empathetic, but we probably shouldn't say "I understand." because her initial thought might be, "How could you?"**

As the days after death add up, aware that there is much to do, it is common for a widow to look for diversions. Some quickly go back to work. Others focus on things like house remodeling, and even to some extent, handling the next steps on the financial front can become diversions. While diversions can be somewhat helpful, they can also be detrimental as they may delay the grieving process. Even in the case of a lengthy illness where she has been in grief for some time, there is still much to process and avoidance or delaying the process isn't healthy.

The days after the funeral are said to be sometimes even more difficult than the funeral itself. The friends and family have left, it's quiet in the house, she wanders through their home and realizes that the stack of bills and mail on the desk has grown considerably. The past is seemingly all she can think about and she is fearful of what the future holds. She feels like she is in control of very little, particularly her emotions and anxiety. She doesn't make a pot of coffee in the mornings anymore. She doesn't read the paper with her best friend, sharing articles of interest. She hasn't cooked in days and doesn't feel like eating much. The thought of cooking for only one person leaves her unfulfilled. Her daughter is constantly reminding her to eat something. She locks up the house at night, but now she locks her bedroom door. Although many of her friends are at church, she doesn't feel like attending as she doesn't want to answer the question, "How are you doing?"

When a widow is struggling with her grief it may be appropriate to recommend a psychiatrist or therapist. **Please see "Is It Time to See a Therapist?" in the Chapter 8, "Resources".** This is a questionnaire that can help you decide if you or someone you love would benefit from talking with a Therapist. If unable to perform daily living activities, then it may be appropriate to find a psychiatrist to prescribe medicine for a period of time to help you function.

This chapter focused on the pain and the experience of a widow during a most difficult time. The challenges that they face from the time their husband was diagnosed with an illness to the death and days after are some of the toughest times to imagine. Many of these challenges may seem obvious and you'll notice that we offered only a few possible solutions. Our intent is to help readers in the initial chapters of this book to gain a higher level of understanding. By conveying the intensity of their situation, we hope we are giving you some idea of the magnitude of the challenges they face and the pain that they feel.

We learned so much through these women and the experiences they shared with us. **We learned just how intense this situation is. We learned that while family support is key, a widow's**

isolation is profound. We learned that doing the little things can make a difference. Bring and eat a meal with them. Check on them often and don't keep asking them "How are you?" **We learned to guide them to seek professional medical help when necessary.**

As financial advisors, **we learned to go slower with our process and remember that we may have to ask the same questions a few times as they may not remember things at times. We learned to have more patience with them.**

For grown children of widows, **we learned that it can be frustrating at times but don't get frustrated with your mom going through this.**

As a friend, just stop by for a cup of coffee or a glass of wine. Perhaps you might mow their lawn or plant some flowers.

Remember, grieving is a process, it can't be short-circuited, and it takes much longer than many of us realize.

In Chapter 3, we'll talk about some of the necessary first steps financially, legally and continue to inform on the process of their grief and the ongoing challenges they face.

---

[i] Holmes and Rahe (1967) developed a questionnaire called the Social Readjustment Rating Scale (SRRS) for identifying major stressful life events. Each one of the 43 stressful life events was awarded a Life Change Unit depending on how traumatic it was felt to be by a large sample of participants.

NOW WHAT?

"Do not fear mistakes. You will know failure. Continue to reach out."

Benjamin Franklin

The months following your husband's death present many challenges, both emotionally and financially. In our career experience, and in the many interviews with widows for this book, we heard the word 'overwhelming' again and again. "The grief can be overwhelming." "The future looks overwhelming." "The loneliness is overwhelming." "The household chores are overwhelming." "The evenings feel overwhelming." And so on, and so on. It's no surprise that the necessary financial considerations and decisions a widow is faced with can also feel overwhelming.

Oftentimes the sheer number of financial duties creates this overwhelming feeling. However, the fear of making financial mistakes is commonly at fault in casting a flood of dread in those faced with the sudden responsibility for their (and many times their family's) financial well-being and future. Many women, whether generational or cultural, did not have the primary responsibility for the family's finances as a couple. But now, as one, the day-to-day financial decisions and the long-term financial choices are theirs alone. Good or bad. Right or wrong.

Financial and Estate Planning can quickly become quite complex. We've counseled many widows over the years that taking a breath and simply approaching one day at a time can oftentimes help them overcome their financial worries – and complications. In the following discussion, we'll follow our own advice and outline many of the most important items that should be addressed, as well as, provide a suggested 'pace' at which to move. To help illustrate the 'pace' of activity, we will categorize these tasks into Phases, although as each situation is unique, these artificial phase boundaries can be flexible.

But first, recognize that you can handle this challenge. While some of the widows we interviewed and have worked with in the past were financially well-versed, many were in fact, not prepared to handle their finances. Either way, the common denominator in these situations was the fog of grief blurring their paths. Yet with the right encouragement, support, and team, they make their way through the learning curve and flourish with their newly developed knowledge and skill.

So, what needs to be done? How are they done? When do they need to be done?

Phase 1 – Handling the Immediate Issues

Phase 1 can be a whirlwind and it is very difficult. Generally, this phase will include the time around the funeral and move you toward the probate process. It isn't a time where you will be making any permanent decisions. Rather you will be preparing the groundwork (and yourself) for the long-term decisions that will come in the future.

We suggest you begin by gathering your husband's legal and financial documents. These can include:

Financial documents

- ☐ Outstanding bills
- ☐ Checkbooks
- ☐ Bank and credit union statements
- ☐ Investment company/brokerage statements
- ☐ Annuity contracts and statements
- ☐ Individual Retirement Account (IRA) statements
- ☐ Stock and bond certificates
- ☐ Life insurance policies
- ☐ Pension statements

- ☐ Mortgage and other loan documents
- ☐ Credit card statements
- ☐ Safe deposit box record(s)
- ☐ Trust account statements

Estate documents

- ☐ Will
- ☐ Statement of wishes
- ☐ Community property/marital agreements
- ☐ Trust papers

Business and real estate documents

- ☐ Partnership agreements
- ☐ Buy-sell agreements
- ☐ Real estate deeds
- ☐ Pre-planned funeral arrangements

Single... Not by Choice

Payroll and tax records

☐ Employer W-2/paystubs

☐ Company benefit documents

☐ Social security card and statement

☐ Recent income tax return

These documents can take some time to gather and *it can be difficult* sorting through your husband's desk or office, so **we suggest you engage the assistance of a loved one or close friend to help you stay focused on the task at hand.** Keep in mind, you have many tasks and meetings in front of you and having these documents organized in one spot can make many of these steps a little easier.

One of the first meetings you can expect is with a funeral director. If you and your husband had made pre-planning arrangements, many decisions have already been made. The pre-planning process can include the purchase of a burial plot, casket, funeral arrangements and details, and even engraved grave markers. Pre-planning arrangements can include either advance payment or burial insurance, so ensure you have thoroughly searched for these documents and confirm with the funeral home if you have any question. Pre-planning can simplify the process, but if pre-planning arrangements have not been made, the director can be very helpful in walking you through the process.

Typically, the funeral director will guide you and your loved ones through the necessary decisions including the type of casket/urn, a form of service, music accompaniment, stationary kits, and car service to be provided. The family will be responsible for composing the obituary, although many funeral homes can provide assistance, and most will submit the obituary to the local newspaper and post to their online visitation site if you wish. Finally, the director will place the order for State-issued Death Certificates. **We recommend you request 10-15 official copies as these will be needed when filing the Federal Estate Tax Return, closing bank and investment accounts, terminating service contracts, filing for insurance benefits, and any number of other**

transactions. Of course, additional copies can be ordered after the fact, but it's better to be prepared in advance.

It is generally recommended that you (or one of your loved ones) keep a journal of all gifts, flowers, meals, and any other form of assistance. It can be difficult to remember all the acts of kindness that friends and family provide to you during this time, and without a record, thank you cards will be difficult, if not impossible, to send.

Phase 2 – The Heavy Lifting

Many consider the probate process the beginning of the 'heavy lifting'. The term "probate" refers to the act of validating or proving a will before a court. Frequently "probate" is used informally to reference all the steps in the estate settlement process. The individual responsible for the estate administration is the "executor." The executor is named in the deceased's will and oftentimes the spouse is named as the executor. For purposes of this text, we will assume you, the spouse, is the named executor.

We've witnessed and heard from many of our

widow interviewees probate cases that progress and finalize smoothly, the common denominator in these cases is frequently a well-designed and drafted estate plan that includes open communication and direction to those left behind. **In our previous book, *Sudden Wealth... Blessing or Burden?*, we outlined a critical supplement to the formal estate planning process – the *Statement of Wishes* – this letter can act as a crucial guide in helping one's family understand their choices and simplify the decisions the family will be making in the months and years ahead.**

But what do you do if your husband left no such guide? What if he had the proper legal documents in place, but never communicated the 'how's and why's? Or worse, what if no planning had been done at all? Of course, one of the major challenges in tackling this subject is that each state, and even county, can have different laws and processes directing the estate administration process. An Estate Planning Attorney experienced in your state will be a critical member of your wealth team as you proceed through the probate and administration process. Your attorney will be able to guide you properly through the legal steps necessary. Obviously, all estates are not created equally and those involved will be making very unique and personal decisions.

When you first meet with your estate attorney to review your husband's documents and determine your plan of action, you will likely be asked to bring copies of the items listed on pages 189-190. It's important to note some comprehensive wealth management firms that provide Family Office Services may have processes in place that can assist in organizing these documents, helping to establish your estate planning team, and accompanying or even facilitating these meetings. It can be a great asset to have an experienced individual with you to help you ask the right questions and make note of your next steps. Not only can the family office advisor help you sort through these documents, he or she can help you compile a snapshot of your husband's estate which can be useful when completing a Federal Estate Tax return.

As executor of the estate, you along with your attorney will need to appear before the local probate judge. The attorney's office generally handles the paperwork with the court and schedules the hearing. After the will is accepted for probate, the court will provide you the relevant documents giving you the authority to act on behalf of your husband's estate.

Then the work can start to pile up. Below is a summary, with comments and suggestions, of typical to-do's we've compiled in the past as family office advisors to other widows. For a more detailed review, refer to the resources provided in Chapter 8.

Notifications

- ☐ Contact creditors and publish a notice to file claim.

- ☐ Contact the Social Security Office and Medicare. Most funeral homes notify the Social Security Office; however, it is a good idea to contact them directly to verify if any benefits are due you or the family. Likewise, Social Security notifies Medicare. But to be safe, call the customer service number on the back of any Prescription Drug or Supplemental Insurance plans.

- ☐ Notify credit card companies and destroy

cards. It is also a good idea to check credit card statements for any payments charging directly to the cards.

☐ Cancel club or other memberships if no longer desired. Check monthly bills to see exactly what needs to be canceled. Some private club memberships are "equity" memberships and may have a market value. Others may provide refunds from the date of death.

☐ Contact airlines to see if any miles can be redeemed or transferred. Note that many airlines charge a fee to transfer miles. Others offer the ability to redeem miles for gift cards or other merchandise. Look online, and then call the airline to verify your options.

Taxes

☐ Meet with the CPA to discuss the time frame for filing the Federal Estate Tax return. The estate tax return (or Form 706) must be filed and paid within nine months

Now What?

of the date of death unless an extension is applied for. The IRS will generally issue an Estate Tax Closing Letter within six months after the return is filed. However, if it is selected for statistical review or examination, it could be longer. The estate may be required to file its own income tax return after its first fiscal year. Estate tax laws are complicated. The Internal Revenue Service provides useful information in Publication 950, which can be found at www.irs.gov. However, for taxable estates, a competent CPA or tax attorney is strongly recommended.

- ☐ Ask the CPA about the **Final Income Tax Return.** Generally, if the deceased has reportable income between January 1 and the date of death, you will be required to file an income tax return for this period. The due date of this return will be April 15 (or next business day) of the year following death.

- ☐ Obtain tax identification number for the estate. Frequently, the CPA will file the appropriate IRS form for you. It can also be applied for online at www.irs.gov.

Life Insurance

☐ Contact life insurance carriers to determine claim process. You'll want to determine the policy's death benefit and beneficiary designation. Most policies will list one or more primary beneficiaries and one or more contingent beneficiaries. Some policies will specify a predetermined payout option. If none is selected, beneficiaries generally have the option of lump-sum payments or some scheduled payment stream.

Real Estate and Personal Property

☐ Take an inventory of personal effects and locate any additional account and loan statements. When compiling the inventory, use a spreadsheet to list the item, its value, and who the intended recipient should be (if known). This extra step helps with the executor's final accounting.

Now What?

- ☐ Contact an appraiser, as necessary, for antiques, collectibles, jewelry, and any other significantly valued items. Many items can easily be valued with a quick search online or at furniture consignment shops. However, for those specialty items, an estate appraiser should be hired. Local appraisers can be found by asking your estate attorney, family office advisor, an online search, or at www.probate.com.

- ☐ Contact home and auto insurance company. Some insurers require notification when a covered property becomes vacant. To be sure the deceased's property does not lose coverage, notify the insurance carrier of the owner's death as soon as possible. Remember to notify the auto insurance company if and when any vehicles are sold.

- ☐ Meet with a real estate agent to request a market appraisal on your primary home and other real property, and if intending to sell, assist in locating contractors to help ready the home(s) for sale.

Single... Not by Choice

Banking and Investments

- ☐ Open a bank account for the Estate. Do not close old bank accounts until all auto-payments and auto-deposits are turned off. Generally, the estate attorney (or CPA) will obtain a tax identification number to be used with this account.

- ☐ Contact the bank about joint, individual, IRA, and trust accounts. The bank (or brokerage firm) will change the ownership of joint accounts as appropriate and direct you to the available options for any retirement accounts. Trust accounts will be handled per the terms stated in the trust document.

This chapter began with many instances of the word 'overwhelming' – and reviewing the sample Phase 2 to-do list above certainly plays into this feeling. Not to mention, some widows will have even more complicated circumstances and tasks to deal with, furthering the need for professional guidance. As we begin to look past phase 2, we're often asked, 'What's next? Will it continue to get harder?'. Of course, it depends on each unique set of circumstances, but generally (and thankfully), the nitty-gritty financial and estate tasks tend to lighten as time moves forward allowing widows themselves to begin moving forward.

In the next chapter, we will discuss how these tasks are often affected, both in the short-term and long-term, by the grieving process and offer insight and suggestions on how widows, their loved ones, and their professional advisors can best work through this process.

LIVING WITHOUT HIM

"What the caterpillar thinks is the end of the world, the butterfly knows is only the beginning."

Anonymous

With a team of experienced professionals in planning, investments, insurance, legal, tax and banking, to name a few, guiding a widow through the necessary financial and legal obligations in the weeks and months after this traumatic event, may help her begin to feel some sense of accomplishment as she eliminates items off her "to do list." As their advisors, we need to be particularly careful during this time. Yes, there are things we spoke of in Chapter 3 that need to be addressed. **But we have learned from experience that we can't interfere with the normal grieving process that must take place.** Some will look for any excuse to avoid grieving. They may throw themselves into a house remodel, volunteer to help others with their grief or spend a great deal of time working with or finding a new financial planner. It reminds us of a time when a widow asked to interview us. She was prepared and had many questions for us. When we asked her how long she had been interviewing firms, she replied, "Four years." To us, she seemed trapped by a grief that had never been processed. Now many years later, we hope that she eventually went through the grieving process and found a financial advisor suited to her needs.

The process of taking over the financial responsibilities for the family can be a daunting task, let alone doing it at the same time they are grieving the loss of their spouse. The funeral was months ago, many of the family and friends are gone and it may hit them that they truly are alone. The house is quiet, and they are alone with their thoughts and their grief. Too many of them, the silence is deafening especially during this time. Living without him means going through the grieving process and constantly adjusting while a barrage of thoughts about him are a constant reminder that he is gone.

The process of grieving is, to say the least complicated. The process is as necessary as it is unique to each person. The five stages of grief, as described in the model of Elisabeth Kubler-Ross, are denial, anger, bargaining, depression, and acceptance. Since everyone is different it is especially important for friends and family and even their advisors to pay close attention to the bereaved as there can be serious ramifications at times.

We learned that it is important to not just ask them, "how are you doing?" That is a question that almost always generates a pat answer of "I'm doing fine." We all must do more than that. Ask them if they are sleeping, eating, taking care of their pets. Ask them if they are having any better days. Don't consider the questions as being nosy or bothersome. Detailed questions may help you discern if they are grieving at a healthy pace or if they or avoiding the grief, in denial, or heaven forbid, are suicidal. Oftentimes you may not get the straight answer as they are trying to be strong for those closest to them.

We learned from our mental health professionals that the mental toll of grief is so acute that it can create or acerbate physical illness or chronic conditions like headaches, backaches, stomach and bowel issues, prolonged fatigue, sleeplessness, and depression to name a few. Often it is a loved one like a daughter that recognizes that her mom isn't fine, in fact, needs professional help and will go with her to speak to a psychiatrist or therapist. It is critical for any of us that care about a widow in our lives to not ignore the signs. We may need to make the appointment for her to seek a psychiatrist or therapist. Some daughters had to remind their mothers to eat!

We were also told by mental health professionals to look for certain signs like the lack of ability to function and then gently say as an example, "In our experience, someone who sounds and looks like you do, would benefit greatly by seeing a psychiatrist who can prescribe something to help you get some sleep." Seeing a psychiatrist is extremely important if they are exhibiting a lack of self-esteem and expressing that they feel hopeless and don't want to be here anymore.

Group therapy can be particularly helpful during this time. The participants in a group are there only to listen and share. They are not there to judge. Just as we hope this book will help create some sense of normalcy for widows and their loved ones, group therapy may do the same. Spending an amount of time in group therapy can help a great deal and last anywhere from a few weeks to some who spend a couple of years with group therapy, making long-lasting friends along the way.

You may find that she is embarrassed that you notice she is struggling. She will express that she is ashamed that she isn't doing better by now. She feels she needs to be strong for her kids. She has read books on grieving widows and doesn't feel like she has much in common with their process.

Each grieving widow knows that her family and friends are there for her. She understands that she can seek professional guidance from her pastor or a licensed therapist. She knows there are support groups to help her share her grief. Months after his death, she may fight the need for medication. Her emotions are across the board as she either has started the necessary next financial steps or is in the middle of them. Often during this time, she is working with a new financial advisory team and personally handling legal issues she has never had to handle by herself. She may be fighting with exacerbated depression and trying to hold down a full- time job with kids to raise by herself. She is exhausted and, yet she can't sleep.

As time goes by, most of us will only remember that the husband died. We typically forget how long it's been. It is difficult for most to consider that even though it's been a while since the husband passed, that the widow's stress and challenges have compounded. Time heals all wounds, right?

The tough part is that they want to feel better. They want to be "fine" when they tell you they are fine. They may be desperate to feel fine and can't seem to find their way and perhaps the people closest to them are pushing them to do things that they just aren't ready for. Most of us want the widow close to us to heal and move on.

We've heard from several of our clients who have gone through this and often they hear from someone in their network that it is ok or "time" to date. In other words, they are giving the widow permission to date. The advice comes with good intentions but, how would they know? Do they think that statement is helpful to a grieving widow? Maybe it is, may it's not. That unsolicited advice may put even more pressure on the women to move on to a next step when she may be far from ready. Let's all take a minute to consider exactly how her life has changed and what challenges may be top of her mind daily.

Six to twelve months after the death are a crucial time for walking through the grief process. As we mentioned, this process is unique to each person. Did you know that she may be dealing with the following triggers months to years after the death of her husband?

- ☐ She is in the car running an errand and hears their wedding song.

- ☐ It's time to prepare for tax season. She has

Single... Not by Choice

never in her life prepared for tax season.

☐ She gets home from work after a long week and her feet are killing her. Of course, he would always rub her feet after a long week or whenever her feet hurt!

☐ Her 11 year- old son needs help with his math – she hates math and dad always helped him with his math.

☐ The car just got a flat tire and he always handled the car stuff.

☐ She finds a moment of silence and gets angry because her husband's illness lasted 5 years and took a toll on her and the family. The subsequent guilt of being angry at that makes her feel like a terrible person. It's called ambivalent grief when you have mixed emotions about the death, perhaps that it should have come sooner.

☐ She just received the wine shipment from their favorite vineyard.

☐ An invitation arrived for a dinner party with

Living Without Him

old friends.

- ☐ The holidays are right around the corner and her husband always got the ornaments down from the attic.

- ☐ She needs to send Christmas cards out.

- ☐ She wants to go see a movie but can't stand to do it alone.

- ☐ She tries to uphold the family traditions.

- ☐ His birthday is this weekend.

- ☐ Her birthday is next month.

- ☐ Their 50th wedding anniversary is next year.

- ☐ She finds herself angry at being abandoned.

- ☐ She's home with the flu and nobody to take care of her.

- ☐ The kids are at sleepovers and she is alone on the weekend.

- ☐ Planning a vacation but he always handled the details.

Single... Not by Choice

- ☐ Your husband's college just won the national championship and he's not here to enjoy it. He also proposed to you at one of their games.

- ☐ His college alumni association keeps calling the house asking for him. Even though you told them he's deceased.

- ☐ On her daily walk, she sees a dog that looks like the first dog they adopted together.

- ☐ She smells a certain cologne and it smells just like his favorite cologne.

- ☐ Her daughter is getting married next year and asked her mom to walk her down the aisle.

- ☐ He has voice mail messages on their telephone and continues to get various messages.

- ☐ Junk mail continues to come to their house in his name.

Who can they share these triggers with? Many of us wouldn't understand. They can't even share this with their children as they feel they need to stay strong for them.

We could probably fill pages of triggers if we wanted to. The idea is that most people truly don't understand the magnitude of their grief and the constant reminders throughout the subsequent weeks and months and yes even years! **If we knew how many triggers are possible, perhaps we wouldn't be giving unsolicited advice.** And knowing about the constant noise they may hear in the head, perhaps the best thing we can do is sit with them in supportive silence? Perhaps that should be our gift? The gift of supported silence.

YOUR *NEW* NORMAL

"Courage is resistance to fear, mastery of fear –
not absence of fear."

Mark Twain

Time goes by and at some point, whether that is many months or a few years, a widow's "new normal" begins to take shape. Some of this new normal is created by choice, new experiences, and new relationships, and some of it evolves over the months and years since the death of her husband. The fear of the unknown begins to dissipate as the unknown was the norm for a long time. Now many of those unknowns are familiar. Every widow's journey toward "normal" carries its own twists and turns often without the help of their usual support group.

According to Widow's Hope[ii], on average **75% of the survivor's support base is lost following the loss of a spouse.** This includes loss of support from family and friends. There are a multitude of reasons for losing friends and family including loss of couples' friends. Those widowed can isolate themselves and at times can be sad and difficult to be around. Many people are uncomfortable with grief and don't want to sit with a widow in her grief or are unsympathetic to the triggers that often accompany grief for many years. Many widows struggle with knowing that it is still okay to ask for support from friends and family without feeling ashamed or guilty that they aren't self-sufficient yet, so instead they pull away. Many times, we heard that couples' friends drifted as the other wives shockingly felt uncomfortable or threatened to have a "single" woman near their husbands.

So how do they deal, how do they heal? It seems almost insurmountable. And yet they do. Some truly do find healing by going back to work. By spending time with their family, by continuing to raise a family. They find that some members of their family and friends are better listeners than others. Some of them travel. Many of them journal. They find new friends. They begin to learn they need supported silence. They find that in group therapy that they are pretty good listeners too, and that makes them feel better.

They may continue to hear his voice and have active conversations with him, ever curious about where he is and if he can hear or see her. In the TV Series, *This is US*, Rebecca is confident that years after Jack's death, he finds a way to make her smile as she feels his presence.

They may be able to share and no longer feel like they are saying the same things over and over. They may have put into action some of the tips or advice they valued. One person told us that it was important that she always keeps her eyes forward, literally keep her "chin up." She said initially it felt odd, but it eventually became a habit and even years later, makes her feel good every day.

Single… Not by Choice

At this point the insensitive or ignorant things people say like "Are you dating yet?" or "Everyone has to move on." or even "Did he have life insurance?" (according to LIMRA's life insurance barometer 2013 only 62% of them did) begin to happen far less often, and if they do happen don't seem to hurt as much as they used to. The unsolicited advice that people with good intentions give widows is typically not useful. Dr. Michael Lerner states in "The Difference Between Healing and Curing," telling people who are hurting to focus on the right/positive things in life is extremely unhelpful. He writes: "It is much healthier, much more healing, to allow yourself to feel whatever is coming up in you and allow yourself to work with that anxiety, depression, grief."

Cleaning out his closet and personal items, while traumatic, was eased somewhat by sharing the task with a family member or close friend and is becoming more of a distant memory. There is no longer a blank spot in that closet as the clothes and other items have filled in. At this point, many shared that they no longer were locking their bedroom door at night and have managed to sleep on more of the bed instead of just "her side." Some still sleep with the TV on or a night light down the hall and some took medication for years to help them get a full night's sleep. Each new day provided new challenges and each challenge made her stronger, more independent and one step closer to realizing that even though she still misses her partner, she knows she can do this.

Many widows stayed in the same house they shared with their husband and a good number of them decided to move into a new place. They couldn't bear the constant memories. The ones that stayed couldn't imagine living anywhere else and maintaining normalcy for their children was key. Several of them remodeled their house or made changes that they both were going to do or that she wanted to do but could never agree on with her husband.

The routines clearly have changed. Cherished personal daily routines like reading the morning paper together or running together are routines that she continues alone but the void is obvious. At some point, these routines can become soothing reminders of her husband and their life together.

Single... Not by Choice

There still are times when these routines can leave her feeling lonely and can act as another trigger, but hopefully, the intensity and occurrence of those triggers diminishes over time.

Like her old normal, the new normal isn't devoid of its challenges. **The journey to normal is complicated and messy without a roadmap.** She still has to understand and maintain tolerance toward triggers that temporarily bring back grief. Many widows still have a young family to raise as a single mother. Just as widows grieve in their own personal way, so do their children. We know from personal experience that the new and increased demands on the mother can be so overwhelming that she displaces some of the responsibilities on one of her children. While many children are capable of stepping up in certain situations, it could definitely harm the equilibrium of the family and the mental well-being of the child. Even so, sometimes there are no other options.

The silent promise she maintains to her husband that she and their family will be okay can create a tremendous amount of pressure on her. While dealing with her own grief she must be aware of the process each of her children is experiencing. Too often we've experienced kids that will avoid the grieving process. We've seen them angry and not able to express why. We've seen them push against the idea of therapy. Often, they want to be strong for their mom, but express it with their silence. They don't want to add problems for their mother, while often struggling at school, especially with their friends who don't typically understand the magnitude of grief and can seem insensitive.

The new normal still has triggers of events like Father's Day and Christmas and their wedding anniversary and the anniversary of his death. High School and college graduations and Family Weddings make it glaringly apparent who is missing. Even years later these moments, can trigger an emotion so profound it makes them feel like it happened yesterday. The shadow of grief can still linger even on her sunniest days.

As part of their new normal many of the women we spoke with had a distinct opinion on dating. They were either interested in dating or not. Some of the widows who had been married the longest stated that they were not ever going to date, had no interest. Others weren't as against it but were not doing anything active to facilitate a dating atmosphere around them nor would they be opposed if someone asked them on a date. The widows with younger grown kids seemed more likely to date. They were opened to starting a new normal with someone else and were open to love again. Some of the women said that a man would have to drop in their laps for them to remarry and it often happened just that way! Sometimes their kids were open to their mom dating and possible remarrying. Few children were adamantly opposed to the idea. That didn't stop the kids from taking a long look at anyone mom brought home. The comparisons to their father were, of course, the litmus test.

For those that did remarry, they faced challenges of yet another new normal often in times right after they were comfortable with the other new normal. Trying to honor their husband's memory, comparisons to their first husband were common, how they each would handle things, how the new husband related to the family and her interactions with his family were part of her new normal, while at times triggering one of the old emotions. It's something they would be challenged with from time to time.

In spite of all the challenges of the new normal, it's imperative that a widow take care of herself. According to the American Public Health Journal, the death of a spouse is a significant threat to health and poses a substantial risk of death. Most women leave themselves last in the hierarchy of their responsibilities especially as a widow with children. At this point, she may be working out of the home for the first time AND raising the family. If she is older it is common to wonder who will take care of her in her old age or if she is sick or injured.

The outside world offers the typical challenges in her new normal. The challenge of feeling their loneliest when in big groups like at football games or parties or school functions. In this regard, we were told that the second and third years can be just as hard as the first. While they begin to enjoy their independence and doing what they want when they want without having to clear it with a husband, the tradeoff is that they can often feel like they don't have anyone watching over them, making sure that they are ok.

All along the new normal, the stages of grief, Kubler-Ross will happen at its own time for everyone and not necessarily in order. Perhaps this is one of the things most people truly don't understand that it isn't a weakness to fall back into depression after making much progress. One of the most significant signs of healing is being able to label these difficult emotions and realize that they will continue to change, but the key is realizing that it is a temporary feeling for that moment only and it is something that every widow experiences throughout the grieving process.

The new normal can bring hope, peace and new adventures. The new normal is also the time to begin to look at your future and yes that includes the necessary next steps that will be discussed in the next chapter. One of the most difficult challenges we heard in finding that peace of the new normal is how to "move forward" while not forgetting the memory of their husband. Moving on or moving forward can be a scary concept to these women. Almost all of them we interviewed mentioned remembering him or honoring his memory. At times without understanding how to move forward, while honoring him, left them stuck or unable to gain peace in their new normal.

Many of them chose to honor their husbands by sharing stories with us and others. Some of the stories were happy that eventually left them in tears as they shared. Not sad tears, but happy tears and satisfying tears that by sharing with others, at some level he was still with her.

Others felt like they were honoring their husband and their union by raising their children with as little disruption as possible. She would make sure that their children were okay and surrounded them with her energy and the energy that he would bring to them if alive.

They would honor their husband by giving and receiving love. Whether that love is to other widows in support groups, to her kids, to extended family, old friends and the new relationships that developed, the ability to be open to giving and receiving love honored their husband.

They honored their husband by being open to their emotions, by understanding the triggers, embracing that the triggers occur because the past love was real and will always remain. They will always carry some pain, but it won't destroy them.

The new normal can be an exciting time, but still filled with challenges and perhaps the greatest challenge a widow faces, like many of us, is staying in the moment. We'll leave this chapter with some of the lyrics from Contemporary Christian music artist, Steven Curtis Chapman and his song "Miracle of the Moment." It is on his album, "This Moment."

Your *New* Normal

> *It's time for letting go*
> *All of our if only's*
> *'Cause we don't have a time machine,*
> *And even if we did*
> *Would we really want to use it*
> *Would we really want to go change everything'*
> *Cause we are who and where*
> *And what we are for now*
> *And this is the only moment*
> *We can do anything about*
> *So breathe it in and breathe it out*
> *And listen to your heartbeat*
> *There's a wonder in the here and now*
> *It's right there in front of you*
> *I don't want you to miss the miracle of the moment*

The miracle of the moment. Well said, the end game for every widow among the many challenges is to eventually be present for the miracle and the "peace" of the moment.

[ii]Widow's Hope. "These Are the Statistics." Widowshope.org. http://www.widowshope.org/first-steps/these-are-the-statistics/.

DEFINING YOUR GOALS

"Goals allow you to control the direction of change in your favor."

Brian Tracy, author.

As we move forward, beyond the initial phases, many of the immediate and intermediate tasks are likely completed. It is now important to reassess and evaluate what your financial goals looked like before you were widowed and what they may look like for your new future. But first, let's take a look at what we mean when we say goals.

Single... Not by Choice

In the financial and estate planning world, when we talk about goals we are often referring to hopes, wishes, and dreams and ways that can help these aspirations become truly attainable. Many, if not most, view this task with much anticipation but also with a great deal of angst. **While it's relatively simple to dream generally about the future, when details are hashed out, it can be a paralyzing activity.** The consequences of decisions are real. The interplay of various facets of one's financial world can be complex. One decision can lead to several more decisions. And all life changes can lead to a multitude of adjustments and modifications. Suddenly it doesn't sound much like wishes for and dreams of the future as much as it sounds like a disheartening chore.

In our decades of experience, we've witnessed many healthy and content individuals and couples struggle with this important financial exercise—even as they are happily looking forward to what the future may bring. As we narrow our focus to our experience working with widows and researching this text through interviews with a number of widows, their families, friends, and therapists, we've

Defining Your Goals

found this exercise can feel so daunting that it's avoided at all costs. To illustrate, we've included several consistent comments we identified in our interview notes and past client meeting notes.

- ☐ "All of our plans included both of us."
- ☐ "I don't feel like I can [or need] to make plans for just myself."
- ☐ "It's just me now, so…"
- ☐ "[Bob] handled all that."
- ☐ "I just don't want to run out of money."
- ☐ "I can't make a mistake."
- ☐ "We had insurance, so that should take care of things."
- ☐ "I need to keep the house… for the kids' sake."
- ☐ "I already have a will."
- ☐ "It [vacation home; new business] was important before Bob passed, so I don't want to change."

Single... Not by Choice

☐ "I just don't want to do this."

You or your loved one may personally identify with some of these remarks. And you can imagine how it's not uncommon for the added burden of grief and loss to add to the feeling of despair, making it even more difficult to embark on this important phase of your future.

So, if it's so difficult, why must we go down this path at all? Can't I just continue to take one day at a time? We believe it's too important of a process to avoid. Consider this. Redeveloping your own goals, assessing your present situation, and determining what is attainable or necessary to reach your goals in the future can bring many benefits. Let's look at some key areas we've witnessed widows find great value and betterment.

Gaining Control

You've just been through—and are going through—a significant ordeal. The situation that began the ordeal was not in your control. Most of the necessary actions (financial and administrative) were not in your control. In fact, since becoming a widow or possibly even before becoming a widow, you have been reacting to many situations without having the ability to direct or control the 'what's next' of your life. You didn't ask for this and it likely interfered with all your plans and hopes for the future.

Tackling the financial and estate planning processes can be a fundamental means of helping you to begin developing more control over your future. It is empowering to be in a position to see the big picture and to not only know where you stand and where you are going but to know what it will take and what type of positive impact you can have on those around you as you continue moving forward.

Adding to Your Well-Being

There are many definitions and interpretations of what well-being means. Most would tend to agree it is generally a state of feeling good, viewing life in a positive forward-thinking manner, and pursuing personal growth. Psychologists offer many ways individuals can enhance their well-being. From simply laughing or starting the day with enjoyable activities to the more complex suggestions such as experiencing and accepting your emotions.

As financial advisors, we've seen well-being enhanced from a slightly different angle. We've witnessed the growth of confidence when a widow identifies her values and can put a plan in place that allows her to find the balance she needs to live those values. We've also seen how a quality financial plan can bring fulfillment to one's life. As an example, a widow whom we have worked with for several years discovered through the planning process that she could afford to stop working and focus her time on renovating and renewing her family's long-time vacation home. The joy and fulfillment she is experiencing from this endeavor far outweighs the difficulty of preparing a financial plan.

Minimizing Costs to Your Family

Unfortunately, the costs of not planning—or worse, of poor planning—can be quite severe. Not only the financial costs but the damage it can bring to your family. Examples of the costs during life could include not being prepared for day-to-day expenses and running out of money during retirement; overspending in the early years of widowhood; not naming someone as your guardian to look after you should you become disabled; or even not having a plan to provide for future assisted living or nursing home care. After death, the costs can continue.

If a person dies without a will, their estate will likely pass to their family. However, their assets could be tied up in the probate process for a long period of time. During this time court costs and attorney fees can become significant especially if the estate is large or if there are disagreements among family members. We've seen many cases, where the disagreements that can turn most contentious, revolve around who should get what rather than how much one should get.

Creating Your Future and Honoring Your Husband's Legacy

What was important to you, as a couple, before your husband's death? Did you both want to fund a charitable interest? Or maybe an education fund for children or grandchildren? Or, if you were just starting out with the hope of building a future together, maybe it was simply keeping the bills paid. Either way, the question you can be asking at this time is "What is important to me as an individual?"

Working through the financial and estate planning process can open your eyes to what's possible now and help you discover how you can achieve your new hopes and wishes while still honoring those goals you valued as a couple.

Where do You Start?

The process starts the same for an individual as it does for a couple. So, if you and your husband had been through the planning process in the past, the steps may not seem all that different. In the section below, we will walk you through the basics and some of the nuances you can expect.

We'd like to start by reintroducing *The Wealth Wheel*. We use this diagram both in our previous books and when we speak to consumer and industry groups about the challenges of sudden wealth. We have always defined sudden wealth as *'anytime you are personally responsible for more money than you've ever had before.'* The key to this definition is not the absolute amount of money, rather it's the relative amount and most importantly, the responsibility that it represents. As a widow, you are likely feeling the same challenges of this responsibility, so we believe the diagram can play the same useful role in this text.

An illustration and detailed review of each of the Wealth Wheel slices is provided on pages 119-137. But for now, imagine yourself at the center hub of a wheel. Each of the slices surrounding the wheel represent different disciplines we commonly engage in sudden wealth situations. The shell around the hub is the primary advisor to assist and guide the recipient as they manage the interrelations of these various disciplines. Assuming you do not already have someone with experience to function in this capacity, identifying this advisor is your first step.

This individual will help identify, prioritize, and make sense of the risks and decisions presented at this stage of your life. He or she will take the responsibility of guiding you every step of the way which will enable you to step back, recognize and absorb the financial and emotional impacts, and ultimately ease into making the longer-term decisions at the appropriate time. It is commonly thought that a trusted financial planner makes a good choice to fill the role of your primary advisor. So how do you choose the firm or person for this important role?

You'll want to interview several advisors from different firms to get a feel of the personalities and experience. **We've provided a detailed list of interview questions in Chapter 8, *Resources*.** Generally, you want to know more than what is on their website. You want to ask the tough questions but be sure you fully understand the answer before moving on.

Typically, after interviewing multiple options, you'll likely hear many similar answers. But you will also start to hear differences that will give you a good feeling on which will be a better fit.

Once a suitable strategist or primary advisor is selected he or she will likely begin by identifying what other professionals will be needed for your situation, many of which you may already be working with. As your team begins to come together, you and your primary advisor will start

Defining Your Goals

down the formal planning path.

We've mapped these steps into four broad categories. Depending on your stage in life, this exercise may look slightly different for each reader. For example, a young widow with school-age children may still want or need to work outside the home, have college to plan for, and prepare for a long-term retirement. But a widow already in retirement may not have the same long-term savings goals for expenses like college and may not have any interest in going to work. In each of the sections that follow, we will provide descriptions that are applicable to all life stages with added comments, when appropriate, for specifics that may only apply to select age groups.

Step One—Assessing Your Current Situation

To gather a fair assessment of your current financial situation you will need to take a thorough inventory of your financial resources including income, assets, liabilities, and insurance.

Single... Not by Choice

Income

It's a good idea to begin by looking at how much money is coming into your household on a regular basis. Consider all sources of income including full-time and part-time salary, bonus, pension, annuity, social security, and other sources. Consider as well what spousal benefits you are entitled to and what changes you might expect of your income levels in the future. For instance, if you are already working, how much longer do you intend to work? Or if you and your husband were receiving a retirement pension, will this pension continue? And, if so, for how long and at what amount?

Assets

Simply put, assets represent everything you own and can generally be categorized into three buckets: investment assets; other assets; and future assets. As you begin to compile this information, consider as well if you are currently, or will begin, adding to any assets.

Let's look at examples of each of these asset categories.

Defining Your Goals

- ☐ **Investment Assets** include accounts you may hold at financial institutions. These could be annuities, brokerage accounts, 401k's (and other) retirement plans, and Individual Retirement Accounts (IRAs), Certificates of Deposit, and even idle cash.

- ☐ Your primary residence, vacation home, business ownership, personal property, and collectibles would be examples of **Other Assets.**

- ☐ Finally, **Future Assets** are assets you can expect in the future. For example, a younger widow may anticipate a future inheritance from parents or the termination of a trust fund. There needs to be a reasonable expectation that an asset will be received before you would include it in your planning.

It is important, for each of your assets, to consider whether you will use these assets at some point in the future to fund your day to day living expenses, your lifestyle enhancements, or other earmarked purchases or whether you want to hold on to something. For example, you may have an extensive jewelry collection that you want to pass on to your daughter instead of being sold to help pay for your retirement. On the other hand, you may have CDs at a bank that you intend to cash out to help pay for expenses incurred during retirement.

For those assets you do plan to use at some point to help fund your retirement, talk with your advisors about likely estimates of your after-tax, net cash received. Say, for instance, you plan to sell your vacation home to help pay for assisted living. Do you expect this asset to grow in value before you sell it? When you do sell, you may have broker commissions and even taxes to pay from your proceeds. All these nuances can change the amount you actually have to help fund your goal.

Liabilities

A liability is a financial obligation you have to an institution or person. What loans and recurring credit card balances do you currently hold? When do these loans mature and what is the rate on the loans? Having a comprehensive list of these obligations will help your advisory team to fully understand your financial position.

Insurance Policies

Now is the time to take an inventory of any insurance policies you currently hold. This would include auto, home, personal liability/umbrella, disability (if you are working), long-term care, and life insurance. By reviewing and analyzing your current insurance coverage along with your asset inventory, **your advisory team will be able to help you identify what coverage gaps or other liability risks you may have.**

As you gather information for each of these components, don't worry about calculating the exact amount of each. It is fine to use reasonable estimates and, if you have current statements, your planner will be able to determine these values for you.

Step Two—Identifying Your Financial Goals

Most couples had long held financial goals for the future. While it can be painful to recall these goals, it is a good exercise as it gives you a chance to reassess what is still important. We've seen many occasions where long-held goals, when reexamined, were not as meaningful as they seemed some number of years ago. Sometimes they seemed important only because they were first brought up so long ago. Time gave them importance, but on their own, they were not really priorities.

However, **some goals, upon reflection, take on a renewed or heightened importance.** In one case many years ago, a widow we'll call Linda, talked of her husband's long-term desire to fund each of their grandchildren's college costs. But given the couple's financial situation and likely long retirement, it was more of a dream than a concrete goal. However, after collecting life insurance proceeds and fully assessing her new financial position, she was able to include this 'wish' as a high-priority goal in her new plan. Linda can now see her grandchildren benefiting as her late husband always dreamed of.

Obviously, goals can also change out of necessity. Widows who previously enjoyed a pension from their husband's former employment may find that pension reduced, or even eliminated. Likewise, younger widows may now have the full obligation to

Defining Your Goals

provide for a young family.

Determining goals, regardless of a widow's life-stage, can seem overwhelming. Where do I start? is usually the first question. We like to start with the essentials or basic day-to-day living expenses such as food and utilities. **In essence, what does it take to 'pay the bills'?** By knowing your basics are covered, you can now build into a more fully-developed list of financial goals, including health care, major purchases, and other lifestyle enhancement goals.

As you begin itemizing your financial goals, you will obviously include the projected cost or amount. But you will also want to consider if it is a 'one-time' purchase such as a beach house, or a recurring expense such as annual travel. If it's recurring, how frequently will it occur and when do you anticipate this expense to end? This is a time where you can begin looking at any and all potential expenditures. Even the cost of providing care for a relative, starting a new business, or leaving a bequest to your children.

Single... Not by Choice

Step Three—Identifying Your Financial Risks

One of the priorities for your planning team should be to help you identify what financial risks you may be exposed to. There are different types of financial risks including those generally mitigated with insurance or legal planning and those addressed through careful analysis and monitoring of current and future spending plans.

By understanding what assets you own and what activities may be involved with these assets, your team can determine if it might be beneficial to increase insurance coverage or even change the ownership of a specific asset. For example, years ago a widow shared with us information about a beach house she owned personally. She loved seeing her grandkids and many of their friends enjoy the property and all the water toys she had on the property. Everything from surfboards to kayaks. Her advisory team recognized that she could potentially be sued if one of her family's guests injured themselves. Her attorney was able to draft documents to allow her to transfer ownership to a separate entity and her property insurance specialist coordinated her liability coverage with this new entity. This was a relatively simple (and common) exercise that helps her manage some of her liability risks.

Not all risks are brought on by exposure. Often widows are presented with windfalls from life insurance or even asset liquidation proceeds. As you've read throughout this book, there can be a tendency to over-gift or over-spend. The feeling of a large sum of available funds can skew the long-term need for fiscal prudence. One of the primary purposes of reviewing your resources and developing your goals is to help identify cash flow risks. By stepping back and taking a look at the effect of 'buying a new condo for a child/grandchild' (or whatever the perceived cash need is), you can more fully understand what it might mean to your future. No one wants to be a burden on their children or loved ones and seeing that, although affordable today, a large purchase or gift might be very damaging years down the road.

Step Four—Assessing Your Estate Plan

The formal estate planning process involves the strategy, drafting, and execution of your estate planning documents. The process has important implications regarding your wishes upon your death or incapacity, as well as, financial and estate tax consequences.

You've seen this importance throughout this text and possibly through your personal estate settlement of your husband's estate. Estate planning is about more than just preparing a will. In addition to provisions of passing assets to your heirs, estate planning can help you fulfill philanthropic goals, provide for asset management, protect assets from potential creditors, reduce or eliminate family conflict, and even enhance privacy.

At this stage, whether young or old, it is important that your current plan, if any, is reviewed along with your overall financial picture to ensure it is properly aligned with your interests. Since estate planning can have many nuances, your primary advisor should include a qualified estate attorney on your team to fully discuss and develop your estate plan.

Prior to meeting with your attorney, it is helpful to prepare yourself to answer some important questions regarding your current plan and wishes upon your death or incapacity. Refer to Chapter 8, *Resources* for a detailed list of questions and considerations we've found helpful in assisting our clients prior to these meetings

Last, But Not Least

As mentioned, your overall financial plan is a living document that will need to be monitored, reexamined, and updated periodically. It will be a useful, real-time, resource for your financial team to help you make decisions now and down the road.

Chapter 8 is filled with a collection of resources that can assist you throughout this financial journey. Use these as needed with your advisory team and if you begin feeling overwhelmed or simply tired of the process remind yourself of the benefits mentioned early in this chapter.

You'll find comfort that as you begin to assert some control in your life you will feel a weight is lifted from your shoulders. And as your plan is fine-tuned over the coming years (yes, consider 'your plan' a living document that needs to be monitored and updated periodically), you'll find much peace as you always know where you stand financially and where you are headed.

REFLECTIONS

"There are three methods to gaining wisdom. The first is reflection, which is the highest. The second is limitation, which is the easiest. The third is experience, which is the bitterest."

Confucius

This summary is coming many months beyond our original completion deadline for the book. Why is that? We think it's a recognition of the difficult nature of the topic. So, before we move on to the Resources and eventual shared Memories, we'd like to take a moment to reflect on what we've learned thus far.

In Chapter 1, we shared some significant statistics highlighting the large number of widows in the world and posed the question "With millions of widows across the world, how is it many feel so alone?" Through our many interviews, we quickly learned that while each widow's journey may have similarities on the outside, the experience on the inside is completely unique. We were aware of the financial and legal challenges facing these women. We knew that the support of friends and family can be strong early on, yet often fades as time moves on. We understood, even just the evenings can seem that much lonelier when the house empties. We were not prepared to hear stories of how going to church, a normally enriching activity, could be such a stress-inducing event that many simply avoided it altogether. Or that the inevitable questions a child may face at a new school or birthday party such as 'Where's your dad?' could bring such feelings of anguish.

We continued our discovery in Chapter 2 as we explored the experiences of a widow immediately following her husband's death. The words 'I'm afraid I have some bad news.' may come from an unknown doctor, a stranger really, following a sudden death or perhaps from a trusted long-time caregiver in other situations. But it doesn't really matter. Her husband is gone. A normal day has just taken an abrupt turn for the worst as a flurry of activity overwhelms her mind.

This overwhelming feeling was referenced several times in our interviews as 'a fog', or 'grief brain.' **We learned from psychologists that this fog can provide a widow protection as a coping mechanism.** Something that can be valuable to a widow as many face their own serious illnesses during the months that follow their husband's death.

The step into our world, the financial and legal aspects introduced in Chapter 3, to us was refreshing. However, we know how overwhelming these duties can be for widows. So, as we looked for a simple segue, we followed our own advice to take one step at a time as we developed the chapter. Through the use of artificial 'phases', we walked through the immediate tasks at hand starting with what decisions may be needed as a widow prepares for her husband's funeral, moving through what documents to gather, offering suggestions to help stay organized and eventually moving into the heavy lifting activities. Phase 2 introduces the estate settlement process and the need and value of using experienced professionals to help along the way.

As items begin to get checked off the to-do lists, widows often begin to experience a feeling of accomplishment. In Chapter 4 we examined how this feeling can sometimes mask a widow's emotions and even interfere with the grieving process. The funeral may now be months in the past and while life is moving forward, loneliness may actually be worsening. **We learned how important it can be for a widow's loved ones and those around her to go beyond asking standard questions such as 'How are you doing?" as it generally elicits an automatic response of 'I'm fine.' and doesn't really reflect their true state.** Some widows admitted to using all the to-do's and tasks as a way to hide from their grief. This tactic was validated by our interviews with therapists as they explained that the enhanced loneliness during the period can often aggravate physical ailments such as headaches, fatigue, or sleeplessness which can all be signs that professional help may be warranted. Often support groups can help move a widow into her *'new* **normal'**, the topic of Chapter 5.

As a widow's life begins to settle into a new routine she is presented with new choices, new experiences, and even new friends and relationships. At the same time, she may have lost other friends either from her own isolation or from these individuals being uncomfortable with a widow's sadness. The widows we interviewed had many positive ways they embraced this period. Many began journaling their routines, many began traveling, and of course, many others went back to work. All these activities seemed to help them move forward with tasks they once avoided, like cleaning out their husbands' side of the closet and recognizing their own ways to honor their silent promises to their husband that they would be okay.

We often find that as a widow is moving through more emotional stability we can make great progress toward her new financial normal as well. In Chapter 6, we walked through the importance of developing her financial goals for the future. While we are often presented with objections during this time, once we illustrate the reasons behind developing a new financial plan, widows often move forward enthusiastically. Reasons such as gaining control following a period of very little control, enhancing her own well-being, and even honoring her husband's legacy can be powerful motivators.

However, enthusiastic or not, it can be a daunting task. We provide a roadmap to help widows get started whether they are looking for a primary advisor or simply adding to their current team. Lastly, we revisit the estate planning process as it relates now to her estate.

The title of this chapter is *Reflections* and it's quite fitting as we look back over each chapter, our interview notes, past engagements and cases, and even our own personal experiences. On one hand, it's scary and difficult. But on the other hand, we have many experiences with widows that are successfully working through one of life's most challenging events in their own personal and unique ways. In our minds, these experiences validate why we tackled this subject. And it has been a gratifying experience.

Reflections

We leave you with two additional chapters, *Resources* and *Memories*. Within Chapter 8, *Resources*, we provide a detailed review of The Wealth Wheel introduced in *Sudden Wealth… It Happens*, the first in the *Sudden Wealth Book Series*. The Wealth Wheel illustrates the financial and legal professionals we collaborate with daily as part of our Family Office Services. We also provide several relevant checklists we use daily as we counsel widows and others that have experienced a sudden wealth life event.

Finally, Chapter 9, *Memories*. In our opinion, this is a great way to end a book. **We collected favorite memories from each of the widows we interviewed and others that lost their husband or father.** By sharing these wonderful stories with you, we trust you will learn, as we did, that although the husbands and dads are no longer with their families, the memories of them remain strong.

RESOURCES

The following pages contain an assortment of relevant resources that may be useful for widows, their loved ones, and those assisting the widow with financial tasks and duties. We have found checklists, self-assessments, and glossaries such as these, to be useful in helping individuals in stressful and challenging situations stay on-track and moving forward.

Is it Time to See a Therapist?

Since your life-changing event, have you been considering seeking therapy, but aren't sure whether it's the right choice for you? You are facing new challenges and it is common to feel unsure of how to resolve these issues. Therapy can help. Dealing with the issues that have arisen with the help of an objective professional may help to clarify your thoughts and feelings. Going to therapy, even briefly, can give you new tools to help make the challenging emotional decisions that you face when managing your new financial responsibilities.

We recognize that a simple questionnaire cannot tell you definitively if you will benefit from seeing a therapist. However, in collaboration with our therapist partners, and working with widows and others that have experienced life changing financial events, we have compiled a list of questions that have helped guide many others.

Answering the questions below with 'yes' or 'no' will help you decide if you are ready to see a therapist to resolve some of your current dilemmas.

Single... Not by Choice

- ☐ Do you feel overwhelmed with your new financial responsibilities?

- ☐ Have you had any gift requests that give you a feeling of surprise, guilt, or anger?

- ☐ Have you experienced any changes to your sleep patterns?

- ☐ Has your appetite changed?

- ☐ Do you find it more difficult to concentrate and focus on tasks?

- ☐ Have you experienced an increase in social conflicts?

- ☐ Does it feel like material changes are occurring too fast?

- ☐ Has it been difficult to set limits on spending?

- ☐ Do you have any fear of sharing financial information?

- ☐ Are you procrastinating on any important financial decisions?

- ☐ Have you avoided any social situations due to your financial changes?
- ☐ Are friends and family members pressuring you to 'move on' with your life?
- ☐ Have you noticed a shift in your values?
- ☐ Have you noticed any changes in your relationships with family and friends?
- ☐ Do you feel anxious or frustrated?
- ☐ Are friends and family members pressuring you with financial advice?
- ☐ Have you felt hesitant or fearful of expressing your views or opinions?

Did these questions resonate with you? Rarely have we worked with someone that experienced a major life-changing event that could not affirm at least a few of these questions (if being honest with themselves). The question that is generally posed after reviewing the list is 'Now what?'

As a starting point, count the number of 'yes' responses and use the following scale to help you decide if the time is right for you to discuss your issues with a professional.

1-3: You are conscientiously discerning the changes in your life and may be in a transitional phase that you can manage on your own. Relying on friends and family may be sufficient for you now. As you go through the financial management process you may find the challenges escalating and seeking support in the future can aid you in the process.

4-7: Seeking therapy now will help you avoid some of the pitfalls that concern you regarding the decisions surrounding your new financial responsibilities. This dramatic change in life and lifestyle has presented you with new challenges. Seeking help prior to a crisis state can protect and strengthen you and your relationships.

8 or more: Your answers indicate a high level of stress that is adversely impacting your life, relationships, and possibly your health. Seeking professional support is advised at this time. Discussing your concerns with a professional can give you an outlet to discover solutions and an opportunity to strengthen your relationships through this transitional phase.

The Wealth Wheel

The following discussion of The Wealth Wheel is an excerpt from our previous book, *Sudden Wealth... Blessing or Burden?*. As a supplement to the concepts introduced in Chapter 6 of this text, it discusses the primary components involved in typical wealth management cases. While considering these issues from the perspective of sudden wealth, **we have found these concepts and accompanying narratives to be highly applicable for widows.**

Financial Planning

The impact of an unexpected financial windfall can be tremendous and either positive or negative. Decisions made early on can be vital to your success or, possibly, cause your failure. Financial choices are frequently interdependent, and sudden wealth can complicate these dependencies.

Financial planning is a comprehensive process that can help you make prudent choices. The financial planning process starts with a thorough review of your current financial situation and identification of your financial goals and potential risks. Then, a plan to achieve the goals, while addressing the risks, is developed, monitored, and adjusted over time. The Financial Planning Association provides an excellent definition of financial planning: **"Financial planning is the long-term process of wisely managing your finances, so you can achieve your goals and dreams, while at the same time negotiating the financial barriers that inevitably arise in every stage of life."**

Individuals working as financial planners are

often employed by large mega-banks and insurance companies, or they may work for accounting firms or boutique wealth management firms. Some financial planning practices are operated as one-person planning firms. Choosing the right financial planner is critical to the success of your financial future.

While there are various credentials for financial planners, there is no single regulatory agency governing all financial planners. The following chapters will walk you through important considerations and questions to ask when selecting a planner.

Investment Management

Frequently the first specialty most sudden wealth recipients think about is the role of the investment manager. The investment manager (sometimes called an asset manager) will be responsible for the day-to-day selection and oversight of stocks, bonds, and other investment options. As mentioned earlier, the varieties of investment managers are numerous and due to the sheer number of firms and specialized professional titles, the choices can be confusing. On one end of the spectrum are companies and professionals who aim to serve individuals who make their own choices of what to buy and sell. This might be your typical stockbroker, brokerage firm, or online trading firm. On the other end of the spectrum are the large national firms. While the differences between the ends of the spectrum are discernible, all the gray area between these two extremes complicates matters. In fact, if you asked a hundred professionals to define and explain the duties of an asset manager, you might get 110 different answers! When starting the search for an investment manager, ask yourself this question: How involved do I want to be in my portfolio? This includes the buys and sells, general allocation, and other tactical decisions. If you want to be actively involved in these assignments and have the time and aptitude for financial markets, then a stockbroker or online trading firm might be a good fit. If you prefer to delegate the day-to-day decisions to a professional who keeps you informed but not actively involved, then look for an advisor that can manage your account with discretion. Whichever choice you make, be sure to reference the designation descriptions and review the interview questions in the following chapters.

Life Insurance

Why do I need life insurance after I just came into this windfall? You may no longer have an income replacement or debt repayment need, but you still have long-term planning needs and the responsibility to protect your money. Future estate taxes, product and tax diversification, or any number of specialized strategies fall under the category of long-term planning. Generally speaking, there are two categories of life insurance professionals: exclusive agents and independent agents or brokers. Exclusive agents represent a single life insurance company and typically can only sell products for that one company. Independent agents, on the other hand, may be contracted with many different life insurance companies. One is not necessarily better than the other; just understand that some professionals will have more product options to choose from than others.

Estate and Family Law

With sudden wealth comes more responsibility.

Single... Not by Choice

And with more responsibility, it is imperative that you take the precautions necessary to protect your newfound wealth for your long-term needs, those of your family and possibly of your legacy or of future generations. An estate attorney is critical to better understanding and navigating the tricky maze of laws regarding property rights, taxes, wills, probate, and trusts. Some states have programs allowing attorneys to designate an estate planning specialty. Attorneys can also demonstrate their dedication to estate planning with membership to various estate planning organizations or bar associations. It is important that the lawyer you select is up-to-date with current estate tax law. Whether the attorney practices independently or in a large group, you should feel confident in their ability to answer all your questions and handle your affairs. The office environment and level of customer service should suit your needs. That the office has a comprehensive system in place to draft and execute your plans and documents in a timely manner and to completion is important.

Business Law

Sudden wealth often opens the door to business ventures not possible without a great deal of money. If you are considering investing or starting a private business or speculating in real estate ventures, then a business attorney will be critical to your team. Again, the choices of lawyers who specialize in business and contracts are numerous. Lawyers practicing in larger offices with many attorneys may have the ability to utilize colleagues who practice unique specialties. However, solo attorneys, through personal relationships created over the years, can have strategic alliances and capabilities with different specialty areas.

Property and Casualty Insurance

Property and casualty insurance—protection for cars, homes, boats and watercraft, fine art, jewelry, liability, and other material items—is critically important to a successful wealth management plan. Like the life insurance options, the property and casualty insurance market is composed of both, exclusive, single-company agents and brokers able to offer products from multiple companies.

Single... Not by Choice

Two areas of concern related to property insurance routinely surface for sudden wealth recipients. The obvious one is the matter of the sudden wealth recipient having more, and more valuable, possessions that should be insured. Of course, not all sudden wealth recipients are buying the million-dollar mansions and filling their garage with expensive toys, but more money typically translates to more possessions to protect. The second, less apparent, concern is the newfound personal liability risk. Simply stated, this is the risk that someone might sue you for whatever reason—but usually for their own financial gain. Not only is more money at stake now, some sudden wealth recipients often become more visible to the public and, as such, become a bigger target for lawsuits. Frivolous and petty litigation is rampant in the United States. Prominent physicians, property owners, or entertainers are constantly being sued for very large sums after seemingly insignificant incidents. One of the primary tenets of prudent wealth management is to protect your wealth. And a sound insurance program can play a significant role in safeguarding your new wealth.

Psychology

Sudden wealth events can be conclusions to traumatic events or sometimes joyous surprises. Yet these very different events represent similar new beginnings and an unknown financial future. Think for a moment about three individuals, each receiving a sudden windfall of $10 million—one lottery winner, one business owner, and one inheritor. Each is dealing with a myriad of conflicting emotions. The lottery winner is deliriously joyful and feeling very lucky for making—what most would consider—a foolish bet. The business owner is relieved that the work to sell a business is over but is now lost after selling the enterprise he or she devoted his or her life to over so many years. And a son is experiencing grief and overwhelming responsibility after inheriting his parents' estate. As we illustrated throughout the stories, all these emotions and feelings can make it very difficult to move forward. Counseling can help one understand these new feelings, examine the problems and opportunities related to the sudden influx of wealth, and take action to move forward. It is considered a modern wealth management best practice for therapists to be included in a sudden wealth recipient's professional team. In fact, as the medical community continues to recognize the benefits of a healthy connection between mind and body, the financial community is increasingly aware that this holistic approach can also be applied to financial management with great results.

Real Estate

Sudden wealth may not necessitate an immediate need for a real estate professional, but as one transitions into this new stage of life, various personal, investment, and commercial real estate opportunities (or dangers!) lie in wait. Having the right real estate professional on your team means working with an individual who is not only highly competent but also collaborative.

Real estate decisions involve large sums of money and carry a lot of legal liability. Unfortunately, it is not common for real estate professionals to be included in most integrated financial teams. But the right professional will embrace this consultative role and add value to the financial management environment. The National Association of Realtors

(NAR) reports their membership at more than 1 million (which doesn't include all the other real estate professionals who are not members of NAR!). So, there is no shortage of options. The NAR offers several questions that are important to ask when interviewing potential agents. It's the typical list of "What's your experience?"; "What designations do you have?"; and "What marketing programs do you use?" It is also imperative to determine what business philosophy the agent follows and how he or she will work with other professionals on your financial team.

Philanthropy

Many sudden wealth recipients are inspired to support causes that are important to them at new financial levels. The most common reason cited as the primary motivation of wealthy individuals to give money to charity is simply knowing that their gift can make a difference. Of course, it is also well known that potential income tax savings associated with charitable giving are equally important. To maximize the impact of monetary gifts, a well-designed and coordinated giving plan, as part of an overall wealth management strategy, is crucial. A solid plan should help one nurture assets and allow them to be given at the right time. Many nonprofit organizations offer planning services to assist with giving directly to them. These services can be an excellent resource; however, not all are created equal. Some financial planning firms, banks, and brokerage firms offer philanthropic services too. Keep in mind, three essential ingredients to include in your plan: support the charity you are passionate about, develop a giving plan that is sustainable and does not risk your financial well-being, and coordinate your giving plan to sync with your tax planning goals.

Personal Security

Sudden wealth and large money transactions are oftentimes public in nature, which can put the recipients at risk. Even when requested to remain private, many state lotteries can post winners' names and cities. Lawsuit settlements that end with large dollar awards are always top stories in the news. Even private estates settled through the probate process become public records. Privacy and personal security are real concerns for sudden wealth recipients.

Not everyone that receives a windfall needs to hire a personal bodyguard or station a security officer on their front lawn. But personal security is important whether it's protecting your family's e-mail and social media accounts or minimizing the risk of harm to you and your family. With the right wealth team in place before (or soon after) the sudden wealth event and using commonsense privacy safeguards, negative impacts from publicity can be minimized.

Many benefactors of a sudden financial windfall find they have no additional need for high-level security beyond what their financial and legal team provides. However, for those who find themselves in larger homes requiring more staff and outside service providers, traveling internationally (especially to exotic locales), and hosting bigger events on their property, they do have new concerns. There are numerous private security agencies for these individuals in most major cities. A financial team leader can help sort through the broad array of services including general security and bodyguard services, most personal security agencies offer.

Personal Representation

Depending on the type of sudden windfall received, one might have the need for a personal agent or representative. Obviously, for athletes and entertainers, agents and representatives are responsible for the promotion of a career and for communication and negotiations with team owners and management or studios and producers.

Most sudden wealth events are not the result of a glamorous and exciting sports and entertainment contract! If you're not the next pro basketball standout, why would you need a personal representative? Simple. You may have financial tasks, both large and small, that you do not want to deal with anymore. Bill payment, shopping and other personal errands, gathering and organization of tax or medical records, real estate or property management, and meeting with contractors and designers on your remodel are all forms of personal representation. Many of these services can be handled by a private concierge firm or a personal administration practice either at your direction or at the direction of your wealth strategist. As you consider options, keep in mind, that this person or firm will act on your behalf, so choose wisely. Trust and accountability are of utmost importance.

Personal Trust

Personal trusts are common tools that can help protect wealth from one generation to the next and are often used in wealth and estate planning. A properly designed trust may have helped protect Mary financially from her own decline.

A trust is a legal entity created to hold and manage assets solely for the benefit of one or more beneficiaries. Trusts can be created for many purposes. For instance, some personal trusts aid in minimizing estate tax obligations while others ease the transfer of property to children, grandchildren, and even charitable organizations.

There are three primary services associated with personal trusts: the drafting (or creation) of the trust itself; the administration of the trust; and the management of the assets in the trust. The trust

Single... Not by Choice

document is created by the estate planning attorney, discussed previously, while the administration and management are carried out by an individual trustee; a corporate trustee, such as a bank or trust company; or a combination of both.

A trustee accepts a great deal of responsibility in managing and administering a trust. Your choice of trustee is an important decision. Selecting an individual trustee may have the advantage of lower direct costs, personal interest in the well-being of beneficiaries, and more familiarity with your personal situation. However, before hiring an individual trustee, ensure that your choice has the appropriate experience, time, and resources to manage your trust properly. A corporate trustee can provide experience and expertise to the management and administration of trusts, however, if choosing a bank or trust company be sure you understand the total costs of administration (e.g., accounting, recordkeeping, law interpretation) and asset management (e.g. management of investments, real estate, or business interests). Finally, it is important that whoever you select as trustee, he or she has the ability to manage the assets in coordination with non-trust assets.

Taxes and Accounting

It's no surprise that after experiencing a sudden wealth event, a new layer of complexity is added to annual income tax filing and planning. A highly competent and qualified accountant or Certified Public Accountant (CPA) will be needed on the team. Tax returns may no longer be simple 1040s. You will likely have multiple schedules (attachments) for new sources of income, and your short-term and long-term tax planning will need to be addressed. The largest association representing the accounting profession is the American Institute of Certified Public Accountants (AICPA). The AICPA report more than 431,000 members across the globe. Some firms are large, and others are small. Find one that has the right feel for you and best answers your questions and addresses your needs. You'll also want to be sure your accountant routinely works with high-net-worth individuals and has experience with sudden wealth recipients.

Banking

Regardless of how much money anyone has, a bank is required for everyday transactions. You most likely already have a bank checking account but needs change with sudden wealth. You will still need a bank that can offer the basics, but higher balances may allow for exclusive accounts with lower fees and higher rates. You may even need specialized lending capabilities. Yes, even with a full bank account you may want to borrow money for business or real estate purposes.

Your choice could be your neighborhood bank around the corner or it could be a national mega-bank. Typically, small banks will offer a single point of contact but may lack the specialized rates or lending programs offered by larger banks. On the other hand, mega-banks may have every specialized product you could dream of, but you may find yourself banking through 1-800 numbers and a revolving cast of employees.

Bringing It All Together

The responsibility to coordinate this team of

specialists is highly important. With several overlapping disciplines involved in making even one decision, mistakes, if made, can be compounded quickly and the results can be costly. Having discussed the fourteen disciplines commonly seen in sudden wealth situations, you can see clearly that managing sudden wealth can indeed be a complex orchestration of many different advisors.

Duties of the Executor

If you are referring to this guide, then you have likely been named the executor of someone's estate. An executor is a person selected and appointed as someone's personal representative to carry out the terms of their Last Will and Testament. The person making the will is referred to as the testator.

Many testators, when selecting their own personal representative, view their selection as an honor. Of course, if you are selected, it is an honor that someone has the trust to choose you to determine and deliver on their personal wishes after they have passed. But, while it may be an honor, it is obviously a weighty responsibility. Many will view it as a burden and possibly even a frightening duty. In this guide, we hope to alleviate some of your concerns by providing some background, tips to get organized, and a checklist of the duties that are ahead.

If you've just found out you are named as an executor and the testator is still alive, you are in luck. We encourage you to review their will and discuss with the testator his or her wishes and desires to ensure you understand the terms of the document as well as their intent, wishes, and concerns. This is an important step that can make your eventual duty much easier when the time comes.

Many times, the reality is the executor doesn't fully grasp the impact of this duty until after the testator has passed. Rather, the executor is left to his or herself to review the document and determine what the deceased really wanted or intended. Attorneys and other advisors can help with the technicalities and details, but nothing can take the place of a real conversation with the testator.

The Process

The duty of executor can be a thankless task so understand there is no legal obligation to accept this responsibility. If you decline the duty, inform the court and the duty will pass to the successor or alternate executor or the court will appoint an administrator if no alternate was named.

Should you accept this responsibility, recognize that you are a fiduciary meaning you are required to act in the best interest of the estate. Your duties may begin immediately with preparing and organizing funeral arrangements, continue through day-to-day bill payment, and progress through ultimately settling the estate through formal probate proceedings – the legal process of administering and transferring a person's property upon their death.

Not all estates will require formal probate and states have different laws regarding the probate process, so it is imperative that you contact a local attorney experienced with laws in your jurisdiction to ensure you follow the process properly. This guide can serve as a general reference only and is not a substitute for professional legal advice.

General Steps

- ☐ Order multiple copies of the death certificate. Most banks and institutions will require originals. We generally recommend at least 10 certified copies.

- ☐ Locate the will. Make copies and keep the original in a safe place as it will be used in court should a formal probate be necessary.

Single... Not by Choice

- ☐ Contact an estate attorney. Ideally, you can contact the drafting attorney, but if not, an attorney experienced in the deceased's jurisdiction can help you understand and navigate your role as an executor.

- ☐ Submit Will to local Probate Court. The will is typically presented in person by the executor in order to be formally appointed as the executor. Some courts will require you to be accompanied by an attorney.

- ☐ Apply for an Employer Identification Number (EIN). An EIN obtained from the Internal Revenue Service allow you to identify the decedent's estate accounts during the account transfer and estate settlement process.

- ☐ Coordinate with guardians. If minor children are involved, coordinate and work with the guardian (of the individual and of the assets).

- ☐ Provide notification of death. Creditors must be provided a notification of death and given the opportunity to present their claims to the estate (some states even require this notice to be published in a newspaper). Notification is also required to change ownership of assets and to inform beneficiaries that you have been appointed as executor. Refer to the Notifications Checklist below.

☐ Open accounts in the name of the estate. A bank account owned by the estate will allow you to continue to pay bills and provide care for estate property until it is distributed to the ultimate beneficiary.

☐ Collect funds owed to the estate/deceased. Continue collection of recurring payments owed to the estate such as wages and rents and file and collect insurance proceeds.

☐ Manage assets. As a fiduciary, it is your duty to protect and manage estate assets on behalf of the estate until they are distributed to the beneficiaries. For real estate that may now be vacant, notify the police department to request periodic check-ins.

Single... Not by Choice

- ☐ Manage postal service. If you are not residing at the deceased's residence, contact USPS.com to have mail redirected. You should also have their name removed from advertisers' mailing lists by visiting DMAChoice.org.

- ☐ Pay bills. Mortgages, rent, utilities and other bills must be paid. Pay particular attention to final healthcare and medical bills as these may arrive later than other bills. If the deceased had a living trust you (and you were not the trustee) you should coordinate with the trustee to be sure no bills fall through the cracks.

- ☐ Create the List of Assets. A final inventory of assets is typically required to be presented to close the estate. This will include, among other items, personal possessions, real estate, financial accounts, and business interests. Formal appraisals may be required for real estate, artwork, collectibles, and closely held business interests. Refer to the Asset Inventory Checklist and Special Considerations for

Digital Assets below.

☐ Pay estate debts. Payment of estate debts including funeral costs, liabilities of the deceased, pre-death healthcare costs, income taxes, and estate taxes. If liquidity is an issue, assets may need to be sold. Refer to the Liability Inventory Checklist below.

☐ Establish trusts. Many wills include provisions to establish trusts for tax or other family planning issues. Trusts can be simple or complex and can require detailed recordkeeping. Visit with an attorney to ensure you and/or the trustee fully understand your respective roles and responsibilities.

☐ File tax returns. In addition to a tax return for the estate, a final income tax return on behalf of the deceased will need to be filed.

☐ Consider a Beneficiary Agreement. It is not uncommon for bills and expenses to be presented to an estate after the assets have been distributed and the estate is closed. It can be helpful to establish an agreement between beneficiaries that outlines how these expenses will be handled. If there is a concern of disputes among the beneficiaries, your attorney can advise and possibly draft a formal agreement that can be provided to each beneficiary offering them the opportunity to ask any questions prior to signing and ultimate asset distribution.

- ☐ Distribute assets. As the estate administration is drawing to a close and expenses are fully paid, assets can be distributed to beneficiaries as stipulated in the will. A clear and accurate accounting of all receipts and distributions of cash and assets is important

- ☐ Close the estate. Ultimately, after all estate matters have been completed you may need to apply for discharge to any liability involving matters relating to the estate administration.

Additional Resource: If you are planning to forge ahead on your own, without the help of a probate

Resources

attorney and/or a CPA experienced with estate tax returns, refer to the Internal Revenue Service Publication 559 for Survivors, Executors, and Administrators at irs.gov. Publication 559 is designed to help personal representatives of a deceased individual's estate. It shows them how to complete and file federal income tax returns and explains their responsibility to pay any taxes due on behalf of the decedent. You may also refer to the deceased's state and/or county probate court website for possible guides and requirements.

Checklists

Use the following lists to help identify and organize companies you may need to contact and assets that may need your attention. These are high-level checklists so not all items will apply to your situation and there are other items that may need to be considered.

Gather

These documents can be helpful as you

determine the companies that need to be contacted and compile your inventory of assets.

- ☐ Bank/Credit Union Statements
- ☐ Birth certificates
- ☐ Brokerage/investment statements
- ☐ Business agreements
- ☐ Checkbooks
- ☐ Child support documents
- ☐ Citizenship documents
- ☐ Credit card statements (look for auto pay items on each card)
- ☐ Disability-related documents
- ☐ Divorce papers (including property and other settlement agreements)
- ☐ Employer benefits guide
- ☐ Health insurance policies, statements, or bills
- ☐ Investment records

Resources

- [ ] Life Insurance policies
- [ ] Marital agreements
- [ ] Marriage certificates
- [ ] Military service records (branch, dates of service, and discharge papers)
- [ ] Pension records
- [ ] Real estate deeds and tax records
- [ ] Recent federal and state tax returns
- [ ] Registration papers for vehicles or motor craft
- [ ] Retirement account statements
- [ ] Social Security records
- [ ] W-2 form showing wages for the current year
- [ ] Workers' compensation paperwork

Single... Not by Choice

Notify

After gathering the documents listed above, review this checklist to build your list of companies to notify. Prepare a list with the organization's name and phone number or email address, contact each as needed, note the next steps to close the account and/or terminate the service. Finally, check each item off the list as you progress.

- ☐ Bank/Credit Unions
- ☐ Charities and volunteer groups
- ☐ Country clubs, alumni associations, and other membership organizations
- ☐ Credit card companies
- ☐ Employer and/or business partners
- ☐ Hospitals, doctors, and other healthcare providers
- ☐ Inheritors and beneficiaries
- ☐ Insurance companies
- ☐ Investment firms

Resources

- ☐ Landlord
- ☐ Life insurance companies
- ☐ Maintenance/service providers (e.g., landscapers, housekeeper, etc.)
- ☐ Mortgage company
- ☐ Newspaper and magazine subscriptions
- ☐ Pension administrators
- ☐ Postal Service
- ☐ Social Security Administration and other agencies
- ☐ State health/welfare departments
- ☐ Utility companies

Inventory - Assets

Use the following list to build your own estate inventory. Check with your state or jurisdiction for any specific requirements. Otherwise, identify each of the following items owned by the deceased and

Single... Not by Choice

notate the value of the assets as of the date of death. Certain assets such as jewelry, business interests, and real estate may require a formal market appraisal. Check the deceased's local area for a certified or professional appraiser. For estate tax purposes, it may be useful to utilize an alternate valuation date. Check with your estate attorney or CPA for specific details and how this may apply to your situation. For retirement accounts, life insurance, and any account with named beneficiaries, record the individual(s) named.

- ☐ Air and Watercraft
- ☐ Art, antiques, and collectibles
- ☐ Bank accounts (domestic and offshore)
- ☐ Business ownership interests
- ☐ Business property
- ☐ Deferred compensation plans
- ☐ Furniture
- ☐ Intellectual property (copyrights, patents, and trademarks)

Resources

- [ ] Interests in other estates and trusts
- [ ] Investment and brokerage accounts
- [ ] Jewelry
- [ ] Life insurance and annuities
- [ ] Limited partnerships
- [ ] Personal effects and other assets
- [ ] Precious metals
- [ ] Private loans to family and friends
- [ ] Real estate
- [ ] Retirement accounts (401k, IRA, or defined benefit plans)
- [ ] Royalties
- [ ] Stock and bond certificates on hand
- [ ] Vehicles

Single... Not by Choice

Special Considerations for Digital Assets

As digital assets, online accounts, and information have become a commonplace and generally simplify our lives, they can add complexity to the traditional estate administration process. According to a recent poll by Intel Security, the average adult has 27 discrete online logins. In a 2017 report by LastPass, the average business employee had 191 passwords. Obviously, it would not be easy to include a list of these passwords in estate planning documents. In fact, it's important not to include information like this in a will as wills become public documents once filed.

Although it can be difficult, it is important to consider these assets when settling an estate. An executor may need access to an online account or they may need to remove an account altogether. States have varied laws dealing with access to a deceased's digital accounts so depending on where a company is located, the rules may be very different from one company to the next.

Gaining access to the deceased's computer(s) may be the most critical step. It may hold all that you will need to access their other digital assets. Likewise, access to email accounts is extremely helpful to obtain. These accounts can provide information when compiling the asset inventory and managing day-to-day obligations. You may simply need to provide a copy of the death certificate to the provider or it may be more involved and require an actual court order. Use the following list to help identify which companies you will need to contact.

- ☐ Bank, brokerage, other financial institution sites
- ☐ Blogs
- ☐ College savings plans
- ☐ Computers
- ☐ Credit card accounts
- ☐ Email accounts
- ☐ Health insurance plans
- ☐ Mobile phone carrier
- ☐ Mortgage providers

Single... Not by Choice

- ☐ Online subscriptions
- ☐ Pharmacy accounts/online prescription plans
- ☐ Photo storage sites
- ☐ Retirement plans
- ☐ Social networking sites
- ☐ Tax offices
- ☐ Travel (hotel and air) accounts
- ☐ Utility and other companies
- ☐ Web hosting services
- ☐ Websites

Inventory - Liabilities

Identify and record the details and values of the deceased's liabilities as of the date of death. Include any joint obligors (borrowers).

- ☐ Business loans (sole proprietor and/or

personal guarantees)

- ☐ Credit cards
- ☐ Lines of credit
- ☐ Mortgages
- ☐ Personal loans
- ☐ Vehicle loans

Pitfalls to Consider (and Avoid!)

Through many years of experience with estate administration, professionally and personally, we've seen our share of complications arise in the administration process. While most administrations seem to move along without major problems, the following items are a few final suggestions that may improve your executor experience.

- ☐ Don't procrastinate. The probate process has deadlines that need to be followed. Do not wait until the last minute to start the process. Delays and extensions could lead to negative outcomes such as tax penalties or even disputes among the beneficiaries.

- ☐ Communicate early (and often). It is imperative that beneficiaries and others with a vested interest in the settlement process are kept informed. Tensions, grief, and frankly, greed, can lead to distrust and conflict. Beneficiaries do not need to be updated daily, but a periodic update on the progress can do wonders in alleviating these concerns.

- ☐ Get educated. These guides are a great start. Don't hesitate to consult with an advisor, attorney, and/or CPA to work with you through the process.

- ☐ Pay attention to all assets. Often, it's easy to 'forget' about an out-of-state property or assume an investment account is being managed. As a fiduciary, it is your responsibility to ensure all estate assets are prudently managed and looked after until final distribution.

Resources

- ☐ Don't ignore the inventory. The inventory can be an arduous task but don't make assumptions about what is important and what is not. You never know what item a beneficiary may consider of value (material or emotional value).

- ☐ Keep accurate records. Failing to keep records including estate inventories, expenses, and major decisions can lead to questions and suspicions and even legal issues.

- ☐ Close the estate. You will need to discharge your liability when all duties are done. Don't assume that just because you closed the bank accounts that the estate is legally closed. Also, consider preparing a Beneficiary Settlement Agreement that outlines how future expenses and or issues will be handled.

Building Your Team

In *Sudden Wealth… The Workbook and Journal*, we provided a detailed set of worksheets to help readers through many of the challenges they are facing as recipients of a financial windfall. Topics ranging from how to find your primary advisor, how to prepare for your first meeting, and helpful aids to optimize the general planning process.

On the following pages, we have provided a summary of the key elements of these useful resources. For the reader that already has a quality team in place, these checklists and worksheets can serve as means to review progress and reaffirm your choices. For those going it alone or still yet to build a team, these resources can aid you in your journey.

Finding Your Primary Advisor

With newfound financial responsibilities, it is important to identify a primary advisor, possibly yourself, a friend, or a professional. This strategist will help identify, prioritize, and make sense of the risks and decisions you may now be facing. He or she will take the responsibility of guiding you every step of the way which will enable you to step back, recognize and absorb the financial and emotional impacts, and ultimately ease into making the longer-term decisions at the appropriate time.

Can you handle all the interrelated aspects of financial management by yourself? Do you need the help of a friend or family member? Or is your situation better suited for a professional's guidance? These are important questions to consider. We've provided two question sets below to help guide you through this decision.

The DIY Approach

Some individuals will want to consider the possibility of themselves, a family member, or even a friend fulfilling the strategist role. To assist in these

cases, we have provided a set of questions to ask yourself when determining if you, a friend, or a family member are qualified to take on this important role. Take a moment to review this list and jot down your thoughts for each potential candidate.

- ☐ Am I/are they qualified to handle these financial responsibilities?
- ☐ Have I/they handled money like this before? If so, how did it turn out?
- ☐ Do I/they understand which other professionals I may need?
- ☐ Do I/they want to do this?
- ☐ Do I/they have the time for all that is involved?
- ☐ Are there any potential conflicts of interest?
- ☐ How do I evaluate my/their results?
- ☐ Can I trust myself/them?

The Professional Approach

If you determine your situation is better suited for professional support, interview multiple firms before settling on the best fit for you. For each firm interviewed, note the interview date along with the names of all meeting attendees and ask (at the very least) the following questions. Ensure you receive specific answers and record the responses.

- ☐ What's important for me to know about your firm?

- ☐ Have you had clients in similar situations and would they be willing to share their story with me?

- ☐ What licenses, designations and credentials do you maintain and how often do you have to update them with continuing education?

- ☐ What was the last continuing education course that you found interesting?

- ☐ Have you ever been disciplined by a government or regulatory agency? Provide details.

Single... Not by Choice

- [ ] How is your firm organized?
- [ ] Is it an independent firm?
- [ ] Who oversees compliance duties?
- [ ] What is your financial planning philosophy?
- [ ] What is your investment philosophy?
- [ ] Who specifically will I work with at your firm?
- [ ] How do you see us working together?
- [ ] How and in what ways will my plan be implemented?
- [ ] Who will take the responsibility for ensuring implementation stays on track- me or you?
- [ ] How do you charge for your services (fee, commission, both)?
- [ ] What is your fee schedule or structure?
- [ ] Do you have production goals or quotas? If so, who monitors this?

- ☐ Are you encouraged to sell any specific products?

- ☐ How often will we meet?

- ☐ What will our meetings include?

- ☐ Record any other general comments and observations.

Final Thoughts

Each question provided in these lists requires an honest and detailed answer. By consistently asking these questions of yourself and of every firm/advisor you interview, you should be well prepared to make an educated decision on whether to go it alone, enlist the help of a friend, or hire a professional.

Either way, it is imperative that you stay involved, educated and up to date as the years go by and maintain the partnership with your advisor. Ask questions, be curious. It's okay to have trust in your advisors, but that doesn't mean you turn a blind eye to everything they are saying or doing.

Finding Your Estate Planning Attorney

A key long-term member of your advisory team will likely be an estate planning attorney. Responsible for drafting and executing important legal documents, this member will also play an important role in identifying and addressing potential financial risks to your estate, planning for your incapacity, and ultimately facilitating the passing of your assets upon your death.

Your primary advisor should assist in identifying and interviewing candidates for this key role. Alternatively, you may already have a good working relationship with an estate attorney after working through the probate process of your late husband. Either way, it is important to have a consistent method in evaluating candidates before settling on your best fit. For each attorney interviewed, note the interview date along with the names of all meeting attendees and ask (at the very least) the following questions. Ensure you receive specific answers and record the responses.

☐ Tell me your experience with clients who are recent widows.

Single... Not by Choice

- [ ] Are you willing to work with my other advisors to achieve the best possible result for me?

- [ ] How do you charge for your work? Hourly? Flat fee? Some combination?

- [ ] Have your documents been reviewed by the IRS in an examination or audit? If so, was the outcome successful?

- [ ] What is your business continuity plan? What happens if something happens to you?

- [ ] Can you help with all my legal needs?

- [ ] Can you or others in your firm help with business transactions, real estate ventures, litigation, and other legal matters?

- [ ] What do you perceive to be the most important aspects of the work that you would perform for me?

Finding Your Tax Advisor

A tax advisor, typically a Certified Public Accountant (CPA), is generally a long-term team member. A tax advisor's work may be as simple as preparing your annual federal tax return or quite complex accounting for business entities, real estate ventures, or complicated corporate benefit plans, to name a few. As was the situation with your estate planning attorney candidates, your primary advisor should help you identify and interview CPAs that may be a good fit for your situation.

For each CPA or tax advisor interviewed, note the interview date along with the names of all meeting attendees and ask (at the very least) the following questions. Ensure you receive specific answers and record the responses.

- ☐ Tell me your experience with clients who are recent widows.

- ☐ Are you willing to work with my other advisors to achieve the best possible result for me?

- ☐ How do you charge for your work?

Hourly? Flat fee? Some combination?

☐ Have you worked with the IRS in an examination or audit? If so, was the outcome successful?

☐ What is your business continuity plan? What happens if something happens to you?

☐ Can you help with all my tax and accounting needs?

☐ What do you perceive to be the most important aspects of the work that you would perform for me?

Financial Discovery

If you have determined the DIY route is best for your situation, use the following checklists to ensure you do not overlook any important areas. Alternatively, if you plan to utilize the services of a professional financial planner or strategist, your first meeting will likely be focused on discovery. Your planner may provide you a paper or online questionnaire requesting detailed financial information. But if not, use the following checklists to prepare in advance of your first meeting. This extra effort will help you maximize your time and value in that meeting.

Personal History

Your planner will need to know basic personal and family information. Of course, this would include your name, address, and contact details; but your full history will include more personal questions such as date of birth, Social Security Number, possibly personal health information, and names of your children, grandchildren, other dependents.

Single... Not by Choice

Financial Documents

- ☐ Your planner will need to examine your current financial documents. Some of the most commonly requested documents are listed below. Gather these items prior to your discovery meeting.

- ☐ Account statements including, bank accounts, investment accounts, retirement accounts, deferred compensation, personal trust, and other financial accounts.

- ☐ Life insurance policies and the latest annual statements along with any current insurance proposals.

- ☐ Disability and long-term care insurance policies, including benefit details.

- ☐ Business ownership documents such as partnership agreements, buy-sell agreements, and business financial statements.

- ☐ Current estate-planning documents

including your will, power of attorney, and any trust agreements.

☐ Latest personal income tax return including schedules and worksheets.

☐ Current income detail, such as annual salary and bonus, royalties, or social security and pension payments.

☐ Future income projections including Social Security and pension estimates.

Financial Statement and Inventory Worksheets

With the proliferation of personal finance software, many individuals can quickly print a net-worth statement or current balance sheet that lists financial account balances. However, your planner will need to know more than just what is owned or owed. He or she is also looking for areas of risk and exposure in your current financial situation.

Some examples of information your planner will be looking for that are not clear from your net-worth statement could include the following:

☐ Are your assets owned by you

individually, or jointly with another individual?

☐ Does your business ownership expose you to unexpected personal liability?

☐ Is your wealth at risk of being depleted prematurely due to extended long-term care expenses?

☐ Are your charitable gifts in line with your legacy goals?

These questions, and more, are all potentially important to your long-term wealth preservation and growth plans, so take them seriously and help your planner gather the appropriate information. Completing the financial inventory worksheet provided on the following pages will help you prepare for your planning meetings.

Balance Sheet

Prepare a list of your assets and liabilities. Indicate whether each asset is titled separately in the name of you, your spouse, jointly, or in another entity such as a Trust, LLC, or Partnership. And list the obligor for each of your loans.

Assets

Be sure to list bank and investment accounts, retirement accounts, real estate, business interests, autos, watercraft, collectibles, and other significant assets. It's okay to keep it simple. In fact, we've seen plenty of listings such as this that work perfectly well.

- ☐ *My Home, Sylvia, $1.2 million*
- ☐ *Beach Condo, Living Trust, $625,000*
- ☐ *Art Collection, Sylvia, $250,000*
- ☐ *1st State Bank & Trust, Sylvia, $900,000*
- ☐ *Cash, Sylvia, $125,000*
- ☐ *Acme Corp 401k, Roger, $1.9 million*
- ☐ *Etc.*

Liabilities

Gather detail on any loans or debt that you have outstanding. Include items such as your mortgage, car loans, student loans, credit card debt, business loans you are personally liable for, and other loans.

Cash Flow

It is important to understand not only how much money you receive monthly (or annually), but also from where it originates and how long might it last. Likewise, having clarity about your spending patterns is equally important. By knowing these two values, you (or your planner) can determine your monthly income surplus or shortfall and help you plan for either situation. Use the following checklists to build your own Personal Income and Spending Summary.

Income

- ☐ Salary and Bonus or 1099 Income
- ☐ Investment Income (dividends and interest)
- ☐ Rental Income
- ☐ Commercial Income
- ☐ Social Security
- ☐ Pension
- ☐ Alimony
- ☐ Other Income

Total Income = sum of all income categories

Spending

- ☐ Housing (mortgage, rent)
- ☐ Property Insurance and Taxes
- ☐ Utilities, Association Fees, Maintenance

Single... Not by Choice

- ☐ Mortgage, Equity, and Other Loans
- ☐ Vehicle Insurance, Taxes, Maintenance, and Other
- ☐ Food and Groceries
- ☐ Clothing and Personal Care
- ☐ Child Care, Support, Education, Activities
- ☐ Mobile Phone Plans
- ☐ Dining, Entertainment, and Recreation
- ☐ Vacation and Travel
- ☐ Healthcare (medical, prescription, dental)
- ☐ Medical Insurance Premiums
- ☐ Life, Disability, and Long-term Care Insurance Premiums
- ☐ Excess Liability Insurance Premiums
- ☐ Gifting
- ☐ Charitable Contributions

☐ Other Expenses Not Listed

Total Spending = sum of all spending categories

Personal Income Shortfall or Surplus

To determine your Personal Income Shortfall or Surplus, **subtract your Total Spending from your Total Income.** If you have a **shortfall** (i.e. a negative number) you are spending more than you are bringing in and either drawing on savings or increasing your liabilities to cover your outflows. If you have a **surplus** (i.e. more income than what you spend), you are able to build up your savings balances.

Financial Inventory

The categories below ask for information beyond what is typically gathered from financial statements and spending plans.

☐ Life Insurance: List each policy description, death benefit, type of policy, year purchased, owner, insured, beneficiary, cash value, loans, and original purpose of the policy

- *Name of Life Insurance Agent*

☐ Disability Insurance: List each policy description, insured, tax status, short-term and long-term benefit, elimination period and duration.

- *Name of Disability Insurance Agent:*

☐ Long-Term Care Insurance: List each policy description, insured benefit amount and period, elimination period, and inflation option.

- *Name of Long-Term Care Insurance Agent:*

☐ Property & Excess Liability Insurance: Provide information about your primary home (size, age, type, etc.), autos, including drivers and ages, and any valuables, such as antiques, jewelry, or collectibles. List any additional real estate, watercraft, aircraft, or recreational vehicles owned.

- *Name of Property Insurance Agent*

☐ • Potential Future Assets: Provide information about any future asset you may anticipate. This could be an anticipated inheritance, real estate and/or business sale, or trust distribution. List source, anticipated amount, and potential time frame of receipt.

Preparing for Your Estate Planning Review

When you meet with an estate planning attorney to begin preparation (or updates) of your wills and other estate planning documents, you will need to be prepared to answer some important questions regarding your current status and wishes upon your death or incapacity.

To help you maximize your time during the initial meeting, we have prepared a list of questions and issues to consider before the meeting and a list of items to bring with you to the meeting. Your attorney will review and discuss these and other situations with you prior to drafting the necessary documents. In fact, many attorneys utilize a comprehensive questionnaire to assist with data gathering.

We have found this advance preparation to be very helpful for estate planning clients and their attorneys.

Single... Not by Choice

Questions and Issues to Consider

- [ ] Personal data such as names, address, Social Security number, and employer information.

- [ ] Names, age, relation, marital status, and any special needs of children and grandchildren.

- [ ] Previous marriage information including former spouse's name, date and place of marriage, and cause of termination.

- [ ] Do you have any pre-marital or marital property agreements?

- [ ] Have you or any of your family members inherited (or expect to inherit) any property?

- [ ] Do you own any real estate or other property outside of Texas?

- [ ] Are you involved in any lawsuits or potentially subject to any other kind of claim?

- [ ] Have you established any trusts, if so, who is the trustee?

- [ ] Have you ever been required to file any U.S.

Gift Tax Returns?

- [ ] Do you hold any property as 'joint tenants with rights of survivorship'?

- [ ] Do you hold any custodial accounts, as 'trustee' or 'custodian' (e.g. UTMA, UGMA, 529 plans)?

- [ ] Do you have any safe deposit boxes?

- [ ] Is any of your property held as (or intended to be held as) separate property?

- [ ] In creating your will, consider who you would like to serve as agent for you and/or your estate in the following categories (consider a primary and alternate selection; each spouse can make different elections):

- [ ] Executor – handles your property after your death, pays bills, debts, and taxes, and distributes your property as instructed in your will.

- [ ] Trustee – if a trust is created, the trustee receives and manages property, and makes distributions according to the terms of the agreement.

- [ ] Guardian – has custody and responsibility for your children until age 18.

- [ ] How would you like your assets to pass after your death? Consider family members, extended family members, friends, charities, etc.

- [ ] Are there any special assets you wish to go to specific people and/or entities?

- [ ] Are there any special considerations, such as financial or personal care of individuals, pets, or others that depend upon you?

- [ ] Other common estate planning documents are listed below. Many spouses appoint one another as agent in the following situations, however also consider who you would select as an alternate agent (be prepared to provide phone and address of each agent selection):

- [ ] Statutory Durable Power of Attorney – allows you to appoint an agent to act on your behalf in most matters.

- [ ] Medical Power of Attorney – allows you to appoint an agent to act on your behalf in the event you need medical treatment and are unable to communicate your wishes.

- [ ] Directive to Physicians (i.e. Living Will) – allows you to state your wishes for end of life care in the event you are unable to say what you want at that time and you have a terminal and/or irreversible condition with which you cannot continue to live without life-support.

- [ ] Designation of Guardian – allows you to specify the person you want to handle your property (Guardian of Property) and be responsible for your person (Guardian of Person) if you are declared incompetent by a court.

Items to Bring

- [ ] Copy of current Will and other estate planning documents (e.g. Power of Attorney, Medical Directives, etc.).

- ☐ Copy of any trust agreements in which you, or a family member, are a beneficiary or trustee.

- ☐ Personal Financial Statement (including ownership status).

- ☐ Copies of recent bank, investment, retirement plans, and/or employee benefit plan statements.

- ☐ Copies of any employment contracts or business ownership agreements.

Preparing for Your Property Insurance Review

Property and casualty insurance – protection for cars, homes, boats, fine art, jewelry, liability, and other material items – is critically important to your successful wealth management plan. In advising wealthy families, we commonly find overlooked risks. These oversights can include insufficient liability coverage, risks due to dependent children, failure to update asset values, lack of policy coordination, inappropriate deductibles, and even unintentional liability exposure from non-profit and for-profit boards. If left unchecked, these risks can materially damage your wealth plan. A personal insurance exposure analysis can be extremely important.

When you meet with your property and casualty insurance specialist, be prepared to provide important information regarding your potential exposure. To assist in your preparation for this review, we have compiled the following list of questions and issues to consider prior to your meeting and a list of items you will likely be asked to provide. While this is a comprehensive list of many common questions and issues, your specialist may identify other areas specific to your unique situation.

An insurance broker will typically prepare an insurance exposure analysis that will examine areas of exposure, suggest exposure limits, and provide alternatives for coverage among many of the top insurance carriers that specialize in the high-net-worth market.

Questions and Issues to Consider

- ☐ Family data such as names, address, Social Security number, and employer information.

- ☐ Names, age, the relation of children and other dependents.

- ☐ Information related to live-in or domestic employees, including Au Pairs; Caretakers; Gardeners; Chauffeurs; House Cleaners; Personal Chefs; etc.

    - Are any of these domestic employees covered separately by workers' compensation, disability, or health insurance?

- [ ] For each Home owned (including partial interest):

    - Property address, year built, and type (e.g. primary home, vacation home, condo, etc.).

    - Titled owner (e.g. trust, partnership, etc.).

    - Mortgagee address, loan number, and contact, if applicable.

    - Square footage and number of garages and other structures.

    - Type of construction, roof type, heating type, and detail of major remodels.

    - Does the property have a pool?

    - Existing protection systems and/or services, such as nearest fire hydrant and station; fire and burglar alarms; gated or guarded community; gas leakage or water flow detectors; etc.

- Other existing exposures including earthquake, flood, brush, wind, farm/ranch, and vacant land.

☐ For each Vehicle owned:

- Year, make, model, and VIN.

- Primary usage (e.g. pleasure, business, commute) and typical annual mileage.

- Garage location and assigned driver.

- Anti-theft type and passive restraints.

- Information on each driver, including name, age, and license number.

- For students away to college, how many miles away is the college?

☐ If you own Specialty Vehicles such as golf carts, ATVs, trailers, motorcycles, jet skis, etc., also consider:

- Year, make, model, and value of these vehicles.

- Where is the vehicle garaged or moored or do you trailer the vehicle?

- Is watercraft used for skiing? What waterways do you use, and have you completed any boating safety courses?

- How often is the vehicle used and do you have special licenses to operate the vehicle?

☐ For any aircraft owned, determine how many hours per year and for what is it used?

- How long have you been licensed or are you taking flying lessons?

- If it is fractional ownership, who is the management company?

☐ Personal Liability

- If you or a family member conducts business from the home, be prepared to provide information including the type of business and annual income.

- Do you or a family member give

private lessons in the home?

- Are any family members on the Board of Directors for any for-profit or non-profit organization? If so, do they provide any liability coverage?

Items to Provide

☐ Copy of the Declaration Page from each home, auto, liability, and other property insurance contract.

☐ Personal Financial Statement (including ownership status).

We cannot emphasize enough the importance of properly protecting against property and liability risks. Through a comprehensive property insurance review, individuals often discover improvements and benefits such as enhanced coverage, reduced premiums, improved coordination and/or ease of administration.

MEMORIES

"If there ever comes a day when we
can't be together, keep me in your
heart, I'll stay there forever."

Winnie the Pooh

One of the biggest lessons **we learned in writing this book is that although the husbands/dads are no longer with them, their memories are vivid, alive and well, and each widow and her family want to share their memories with others.** These memories almost always bring a smile along with a few tears.

Single... Not by Choice

We asked widows and their children to share some of their favorite memories of their husbands/dads with us and thus you the readers.

They are in no particular order and are of course anonymously contributed and the names have been changed. When we asked them to share their memories, the floodgates opened with examples of a life well lived and a person who loved and was well loved. Even though you don't know these men, we hope these stories will make you smile and reminisce about the husbands and fathers in your life.

We are honored to share their stories.

It has been almost 7 years since my dad passed away, and it is still very hard to think about him without tearing up. The funny and happy things especially tear at your heart. You want to bury those memories, so it does not hurt again. My dad was an only child and I think that is why he wanted a big family. He and my mom always put the family first. Our happiest memories of my dad are just the sheer moments together. He was an amazing athlete and played both football and basketball throughout his life. He taught me how to shoot and attempted to teach me to dribble. With a large family, it was rare when you got to do something with dad all by yourself. I remember getting to go shoe shopping once with him by myself when I was 8 years old (about 45 years ago!) Sure, getting my first pair of Converse All Stars was cool, but shopping by myself with my Dad was even cooler!

Joe was a big prankster. The kids were always leery of being his current target. Our daughter tells a story that I cringe at, but she laughs. When he would pick her up at a friend's house, he would always yell from the car something like, "Hurry up and get in!" When she would get close to the car he would move forward a few feet. With her friends outside watching, he would do this over and over and over, all the while my daughter was saying "Dad, stop you're embarrassing me!" Well, of course, she was laughing, he was laughing and so were all her friends. It's the dumb little things you remember sometimes! He was like a child himself sometimes!

My dad loved to play golf. He always had a golf club or two in the master bedroom that he practiced swinging. It was a normal thing, seeing him swing two-three times then put it up by the dresser. My mom would constantly tell my dad to stop doing that as he was going to break something or hit someone. One day, my mom and all of us kids were on the other side of the house and heard a huge crash. We said, "What was that?", but mom immediately said, "I know exactly what that was." We all ran to the master bedroom only to find the room empty and the ceiling fixtures in pieces all over the floor. My mom yelled "BILL!!", then the toilet flushed, and my father came out of the bathroom with a grin on his face, and said innocently, "What happened?"

Memories

On ice and snow days, while the kids were in school, my husband would get busy building up snowballs. When the kids started walking up to the house, he would jump out from behind a shrub and start peppering them with snowballs. To this day, the kids love to talk about it.

Dan would pack the kid's lunches in the mornings. He would always leave each of them a note of encouragement. The kids loved reading his message more than the fabulous lunch he would always pack!

One memory about my dad was when I was starting in my 20's my dad would tell me stories about different opportunities (mainly real estate) that he would miss out on or pass on because his dad would always talk him out of doing it. My dad was born in 1930 and the family scraped their way through the depression era which put my grandparents in a 'take no risk' approach to life which is why he always talked my dad out of ever taking a risk or buying anything he didn't need. The end result was my dad never changed jobs and he worked as a police officer for 31 years retiring in 1986 with a great pension and cash savings but only 2 valuable real estate assets (his house and his parent's house which he inherited, both of which were necessary things to own). My dad would always encourage me to take some risk in life and with real estate investments (even though he would cringe if he knew what it really cost for me to take those risks) and it helped me approach opportunities in a different way throughout my life.

My dad would never let me win at any game or sport. He said it built character and perseverance. Even though I hated losing, it did make me tougher!

My husband would put a blanket on his head and act like a jellyfish and chase the kids around the house. I can still hear the laughter!

My most vivid memories of my dad were at family BBQs. He made BBQ the old-fashioned way. He had a barrel smoker and used charcoal and pecan wood. He would set the meat out early to allow it to reach room temperature which also allowed time for his charcoal to reach the appropriate temperature. I remember him prepping as early as 7:00 AM and the finished product not reaching the table until after 1:00 PM. It was hard work and a lot of preparation, but he loved it! He loved inviting friends and family over to enjoy the cookout. He took great pride in serving his BBQ. I must say that I never ate any restaurant BBQ until after my dad couldn't make his special BBQ any longer.

Each Christmas when our kids were very young, my father would take us to pick out the most special Christmas tree we could find. Since we were on a tight budget, it made it even more special. We all looked forward to beginning the Christmas season with this ritual. It was clear that my father got great pleasure in doing this for us to see the excitement in our sons' eyes.

When I was fourteen, my father and his best friend took me fishing on the Frio River. Although the weather was nice for February, it got steadily colder as we got closer to Uvalde in what Texans call a "blue norther." We, of course, decided to brave the cold and fish anyway. After an hour or so of no bites and dropping temperatures, my father and I insisted it was too cold to fish. His friend was determined to continue but finally saw the wisdom in our words. He started to reel in his line when he discovered that the eyelets on his rod had frozen. After a lot of laughter and kidding him about wanting to fish longer, he cut his line and we left to go warm up in the cabin.

Memories

Steve loved to coach the boys' baseball teams. Even though he had a very busy career, he always made time to be head or assistant coach. The amount of time he spent with each boy created a bond that existed for the remainder of his life.

We were married 40 years. For most of those 40 years, my husband brought me a cup of tea every single morning.

I still very much remember the evening that J. proposed to me. He had come home, and I could tell he was giddy about something. He could not resist my prodding and pulled out a box from his pocket. As you might expect, inside was a ring. He had just picked it up. He had worked with a local jeweler to custom design this unique engagement ring with a pear-shaped diamond, his birthstone. It was meant to be paired with the wedding band, also a pear-shaped sapphire - my birthstone. These two rings came together to form an infinity symbol. J. has been planning to propose on an upcoming trip we had planned to the Ozarks but couldn't wait. He did point out the spot when we hiked the Ozarks.

One memory was about 4 or 5 years ago when my dad was experiencing the early stages of Alzheimer's and I took over his finances (other than payment of his day to day bills which he wanted to keep so that he was still independent). After finding all of the accounts that he had opened over the years and getting everything consolidated I was finally able to get the big picture of his net worth. One day I went to his house to visit with him and when I told him that he should spend some of his money and enjoy life he, of course, resisted because he said that he never wanted to burden his kids with paying for him should he run out of money. At that time I asked him if he knew what his net worth was and he said no. I quickly rattled off the money in the various investments and bank accounts along with the real estate he owned and when I gave him a final number and told him he was "a millionaire" he looked at me first with shock and then he got the biggest smile I think I have ever seen on his face and shook his head in disbelief. It was one of the really cool moments to share with him because he never saw himself as anything more than a paycheck to paycheck country boy from Georgetown Texas. Unfortunately for him, he didn't have quite the energy or the health to go and do the things he always wanted to do. (Another lesson for me to enjoy life before I can't.)

Some of my best memories with my Dad was when I was young and would go out on the weekends to help him at the various ranches we had. The horses and cattle always needed attention. Usually, it was later in the afternoon and evening after he got off work and we would usually work at the ranched until dark. Afterward, on the ride home, we would have the windows rolled down in the warmer months with the radio playing country music while the evening countryside sounds and smells came through the windows down the dark country back roads.

My husband loved Christmas. Every year he would give me my first Christmas present the day after Thanksgiving! It always started the season out wonderfully. Each gift was special and well thought out. He would be as excited giving the gift as I was in receiving it.

Every year, over the first week in August, we travel up to Mercer, Wisconsin for vacation. My parents bought a resort in Mercer in the early 1970s and since we had 10 cabins, four lodge rooms, a restaurant and a bar to operate my older brother, sister and I were never in need of finding a summer job. Mom and dad saw to it that there was more than enough work for everyone for the next 9 years, or until you graduated from college and were able to escape.

Faced with the fact that their last child, and free laborer, was soon to graduate high school and head off to college, they sold the resort and entered a short-lived two-year period of retirement. In 1981, they talked my sister and her newlywed husband into moving back to Mercer and starting a restaurant in the small town, cooking the German recipes mom cooked at the resort.

The town of Mercer is also self-identified as "The Loon Capital of the World" and has a celebration, "Loon Day," on the first Wednesday in August every year for this bird. Thousands of tourists gather in town to shop, eat, and drink from the local businesses and the hundreds of craft vendors that come to town and fill up the streets. So, our annual vacation to Mercer in August is what we call our "German Vacation" as several days are spent setting up, working the event, then taking down and cleaning up afterward. It isn't all rest and relaxation.

The day prior is always the time that dad and I load up my brother-in-law's pickup truck with all the supplies we'll need, drive the eight miles into town and set everything up in front of the restaurant. We've done it together for at least the past fifteen

Single... Not by Choice

years and little ever changes. The first task is always to get the two picnic tables onto the truck and then squeeze everything else around them. Dad built these tables years ago and he built them to last. He found the heaviest, thickest boards he could find and once he put them all together each table must have weighed over two hundred pounds. The first table is always easy as we just slide it into the bed of the truck, top-side down. The second table now has to sit over the top of the first and to do that we set it alongside the bed of the truck, dad on one end of the table, me on the other. Putting our hands on the edges of the table, knees bent, we clean-and-jerk the table over our heads, arms fully extended to ensure the legs clear the side of the truck, then slide it over the legs of the upside-down table already in the truck. This year, once completed, my first act was to bend over, put my hands on my knees, gasp for air, and take the pressure off my lower back. As I caught my breath I looked up and there was dad putting more things on the truck like nothing happened. I was 48 at that time and dad was 81!

Unfortunately, within a few months dad would be gone. In January 2011, I was with him in the hospital when one of his nurses told me, "He's the strongest 81-year old I've ever met." All I could do was smile in return. Indeed, he was…

After Jon passed, me and the kids decided to clean out the garage. That was his domain, which meant it was "a mess." The only reason why the rest of his life was kept in order was that he had people in his law office to keep everything organized and me at home to keep the house running smoothly. As we were cleaning the garage, one of the kids was going to be the one sorting the tools. You see, Doc hated not being able to find things he needed, so when he couldn't find something he just bought another one to replace it. One after the other, each kid was picking through mounds of tools when one of them would say "Here's a hammer." a few minutes later another kid said, "Here's a hammer.", and so on…. it became comical. When we'd organized all the tools, we looked down at the pile of tools and we'd all found seven hammers. Everyone laughed because they knew that was something only their dad would have done.

Single... Not by Choice

Everyone kept a hammer that day. We still laugh every time we see a hammer.

Spontaneity is something I'll always remember about Dad. We liked to travel together as a family and a memory that stands out and highlights that spontaneity is a time we took a 'day' trip to Sea World in San Antonio. It was my mom and dad, my future wife, and me. Just a short trip.

It was July, Sea World was recently opened, and concrete was everywhere. Because the newly planted trees hadn't matured to provide any sort of shade, we walked around all day in the sweltering Texas summer sun. It was one degree shy of miserable. We made it through to mid-afternoon before we agreed, enough was enough, and loaded up back in the car for a quick drive home. However, by the time we were back on the highway, I guess my dad got his second wind (or possibly it was heat exhaustion) but he turned to my girlfriend and me in the backseat and said: "Hey, let's go to Astroworld!"

Memories

Astroworld was in Houston, about three hours from San Antonio. I thought that was a great idea because I knew I would just have studying to do when I got back home. But my mom said, "Beau, I don't have a change of clothes, makeup, or anything." No problem for my dad. He simply said, "That's fine. They have plenty of stores in Houston!" as he exited for Interstate 10 headed to our new destination.

I have a lot of fond memories of my dad. The holidays, especially Christmas, provided the family with some really good ones. As a kid, my idea of a Christmas tradition was anything centered around opening presents. And I thought our tradition was solid. Christmas Eve service, dinner, then presents! One year, Dad had an idea.

Apparently, I always tried to figure out what I had under the tree in the days leading up to the big day. My dad was always catching me snooping around. But in the one particular year, he asked if I would prefer to open one present a day until Christmas.

Single... Not by Choice

Trying to downplay my excitement, I respectfully replied "Yes sir. I would very much like to do that." And so, we embarked on what I thought was possibly the best idea of the year.

By the time Christmas Eve rolled around, I had opened all but one of my presents. The evening began as usual, Christmas Eve service, dinner, but now only one present. It became apparent this might be the dumbest idea I could have imagined. My worst fear, only one present, was now a reality. Of course, my Dad knew what he was doing. His plan stopped my snooping and helped me learn to appreciate more than just the presents. And, even though this is just a small little thing, I believe it was one of many small things my dad did that has helped me become a better dad.

When I was in elementary school we lived in a picturesque neighborhood, in the foothills of a beautiful mountain range. I saw how hard my dad worked and, even at my young age, I was thankful to be so fortunate.

He was a banker and enjoyed taking me with him to the office on weekends where I would run and explore all around the Bank. I would tell my dad all the time, how much I wanted to be a banker like him. One time he told me how he got started.

When he was discharged from the Marine Corp, he began working on drilling rigs in the oil fields of West Texas. He hated the bitter cold and windy winter days in the field. One day, he was downtown and passed a bank lobby. He said the folks in there all looked so warm he decided to go in and ask to speak to the manager. When they met, my dad told him he'd like to 'hire out' (rancher's slang for 'I'd like to apply for a job.'). He got the job and began a successful career as a banker.

Something about my dad that was funny is he always seemed to find a way to be involved in, for lack of a better term, a bad wardrobe contest. Nearly every Saturday morning, when I was in elementary school, Dad and the other neighborhood dads would head out to mow the lawn. But for some reason, they had a standing competition of who could dress the absolute worst. I'm not talking about just some old grungy clothes, I'm talking about the weirdest, strangest, old grungy clothes. As a kid, I thought it was funny until I was a pre-teen when I just thought it was embarrassing.

I never really found out what the prize for winning (or punishment for losing) was, but I suspect it had something to do with who had to buy the cocktails. Embarrassed or not, competition day always seemed to end with the neighborhood dads and moms sipping a drink, listening to Willie Nelson, and watching the kids play. Dad was a lot of fun.

My husband cared about his lawn – A LOT. He was so diligent in having a manicured property, that we always kidded him that he was born outside since being outside was his happy place. To this day I just picture him supervising the perfectly manicured properties in heaven.

Memories

So many thoughts that bring sweet memories and a smile to my face! Our relationship was so special, we loved to travel. One special memory of him on the steps in Cortona, Italy so enjoying gelato! His laugh and how he loved life! Every day was a gift!

My dad was a big man, 6' 3" and about 230 lbs. He had a heart to match. So, when I was preparing for my wedding, I asked that he wear a tuxedo. His response was, he loved me dearly, but he was not wearing a "monkey suit." Period! I understood how uncomfortable he would be and let it drop. He purchased a new dark blue suit for the big day.

On the day of the wedding, the women in the bridal party dressed in the parish rectory, which was across the street from the church. When I stepped out the door I saw my wonderful father standing on the steps of the church wearing the "monkey suit" he so adamantly refused to consider!

Single... Not by Choice

The memory of that moment will always bring me to tears. It was then I realized how much he loved me and that he would do anything for me. I miss him so!

My friend Jim and I turned 21 and were heading to Vegas for the first time. As we were backing out of the drive, my Dad came walking out and waved us down. We thought "Oh, here comes the speech." I rolled the window down and all my Dad said was "Boys, remember this. If alcohol made you gamble better, they wouldn't give it away for free!" He turned around and walked back in the house. Wise words indeed!

My Dad wasn't one for giving advice, but he did instill the value of the dollar through his actions. I didn't realize what I had learned from his example until my husband and I had our own children. When I was in 7th grade my family moved to New Mexico

Memories

and took up snow skiing. I have lots of wonderful memories of our trips to the slopes. At the time I wasn't aware of the cost of taking a family of 6 skiing. I was focused on the fun. My Dad made it work by saving money where he could. He began a tradition of us all riding the first chair of the day up the mountain together. We'd then all follow him down the slope. Turn after turn he'd look for the perfect tree well while wearing a backpack full of ham and cheese sandwiches, chips and Snickers candy bars; lunch for the day. "Remember this spot," he'd say "And come back and grab your lunch whenever you're hungry." I've carried on the tradition. I'm sure to stock up on Snickers candy bars and M&M's in our hometown before we travel to the mountains. Why pay $1.50 per candy when Randall's sells them for half the price? My kids have the backpack routine down pat and know a burger in the lodge for $20 a piece is a rare treat. I smile heartwarmingly thinking of my Dad while I take a bite of my ham and cheese. I'm happy to carry on the tradition in his honor.

Single... Not by Choice

Jim had a rare ability to always be in a good mood. At times in our marriage, it frustrated me that he never seemed to have a bad day. And when I would call him on it, "How can you always be in a good mood?" He would always say "Well I'm married to you!" He must have said this over a hundred times in our 35-year marriage.

When I was in my late 30's, I stopped by my Dad's house in San Antonio for a visit before I headed out for the evening with friends. As I was leaving, my dad gave me a big hug and said: "Angel Baby" (his nickname for me) I really wish you wouldn't go and stay out so late because this town is dangerous especially for women. Why don't you just stay here tonight so I won't worry about you."

As a mother, I was taken aback by his concern. I said, "Daddy, you don't have to worry about me, I'll be okay." I thought a lot about what he said and as I was leaving, I said to him, "It doesn't matter how old your kids are, does it?" He said, "You never stop worrying about your children and one day you'll understand what I mean." Of course, he was right.

One of my favorite recollections of stories about my Dad comes from one of his carpool buddies who shared this story at Dad's funeral. It reminds me of his subtle humor, abundant at work and at home, and so relatable since my accounting mind always meshed with his civil engineering way of thinking. The following is how I remember this anecdote.

Dad carpooled to work with three of his engineering colleagues and one secretary who worked closely with all of them. The secretary began the morning ride by sharing with them that she had a 6-foot pole she planned to use in an upcoming neighborhood parade. She further explained that she needed a pole that was 72 inches long and she could shorten the one she had. After a long pause, my Dad responded, in his slow and deliberate fashion, "Well, you better not cut off too much." Dad's buddy told me the other carpool riders could not restrain themselves and all broke into raucous laughter.

My husband had a way of communicating with the kids. One of my favorite memories was when our girls were in their teens. He would tell them, "If you sneak out of that window and I find out about it, I'm going to wax your ass and you won't be able to sit down for a week!" They never snuck out of the house.

I enjoyed my quality time with my father as a young teenager. When the fishing season started we would go almost every Saturday. We would get up early and hit the road. Sometimes we would go to these small brooks or go to the Farmington River. We only went for trout. Our conversations were mainly held in the car because once we started to fish we needed to be quiet. At the end of the day, we would always measure our catch to see who caught the longest trout. I guess we wanted to see who had bragging rights when we got home.

Although this was 40+ years ago I can still vividly see the two of us walking the streams and fishing.

Rick was the love of my life. We were fortunate to have known each other for 10 years but unfortunate to only be married for 2 of them. I would give anything to have one more day, one more year. One of my favorite memories of him was his enthusiasm for life. He seemed to wake up every day hopeful and go to bed thankful. I don't know how he did it but, in his honor, I try every day to do the same.

He will forever be remembered for lighting up a room and making everyone feel important. For being a master storyteller who had a joke for every occasion. The consummate host who made everyone feel welcome. An avid golfer who will be missed by his golfing buddies. And a talented watercolor artist who made sure his children had a painting for every wall in their homes. We have been forever transformed by who he was and what he stood for – it is a blessing we treasure.

A direct early memory of my father is mostly from what I think were Saturday mornings over a few slow-moving years. My father would take my brother and me in the car to visit his friend Oscar at the Texaco station. Oscar owned the station with another man. He was a football player from the 1930's and a pretty big guy. He always wore a drab green uniform. He would give my brother and I nickels for the coke machine or just to save. He and my father would say that those nickels "just burned a hole" in my brother's pocket. I tended to save mine and accumulated a decent cash drawer. Normally, daddy and Oscar would talk about the kind of things men talked about—football, politics, and money. As time moved on I noticed the talk was more consistently about money and what it can do. As it turns out, my dad's friend had sort of a double life. Eleven months of the year he wore the drab green uniform at the station and the other month he would go to Europe and visit his bankers in places like Zurich and Paris. Essentially, he lived off the station and invested in Europe. A long time ago when it really meant something, Oscar had a real money portfolio of at least one million dollars. My father and Oscar liked to call each other "my close friend," meaning they were close with their money. Over their coffee, with my little knees perched on the red back chairs and my elbows on the table, I heard them talk about things like "blue chip" and "stocks." Of course, this was the beginning of the something lasting decades and set up what daddy would do with his money. He had other brokers but mostly he just told them what he wanted to do because Oscar had told him what to do.

EPILOGUE

We wrote *Single… Not by Choice* in 17 months. We completed it 5 months after our original deadline. It was a difficult book to write. We understand the necessary financial and legal challenges that follow a spouse's death and were prepared to write about it and we have. Loss of a spouse is a fairly common form of sudden wealth, so in that aspect, we were well versed in the topic. But our efforts in this book also delved into the personal journey and psyche of a widow. We weren't as prepared for that. The widows who were so kind to share their stories with us taught us many lessons, but mainly that the complexity and intensity of their journey can be lost on those of us who have not walked in their footsteps.

We interviewed countless women who had lost their husbands either suddenly or after a lengthy illness. We felt a great responsibility to them to convey their spirit, their perseverance, along with the magnitude of their journey. We hope we got "some" of that right. Remember, we aren't therapists. Our primary goal was to deliver the guidance on the financial side while gaining a greater understanding and delivering insight about the personal side to the reader.

In delivering the insight of their personal journey **we learned that we all play a role in the process of their grief both immediately and the weeks and months that follow. We learned that asking them a concerned "How are you doing?" is not enough.**

We learned that while grieving is a process, everyone handles that process in their own unique way. We also learned that the challenges of that process are so profound that the side

Epilogue

effects can literally make them physically ill.

We hope you share this book with others. Our financial guidance and pace are sound. That guidance coupled with extreme patience and compassion by their financial team along with their family's constant support will help them toward the healing path that most will eventually find.

Hopefully, you learned a few things by reading this book. If you didn't then you are well ahead of most of us who can now change some of our habits in understanding and supporting the widows in our lives.

We thank our trusted psychiatrists and therapists for being our advocates, our teachers of the mind and spirit, and for providing a safe path for any of our clients who seek their guidance.

Finally, we say a heartfelt thank you to the women who shared their journey with us. While the stories can be difficult, they each found their healing path. And thankfully for us, they all left our office with a smile on their face. We hope we did them proud.

ABOUT THE AUTHORS

This is the fourth book of the *Sudden Wealth Book Series* written by David Rust and Shane Moore. They are the founders and managing partners of Quartz Financial, a firm specializing in the paths of sudden wealth to generational wealth. They have a combined 53 years of experience handling the unique needs of wealthy families. Their firm executes and facilitates family office services for a select group of families, primarily in Texas. Prior to founding Quartz in 2007, they worked in Senior level positions for major banks, brokerage firms, insurance firms and private banking groups.

Single... Not by Choice

David is a graduate of the University of Texas at Austin. He holds the designations of Chartered Financial Consultant, ChFC, Accredited Asset Management Specialist, AAMS, and Chartered Retirement Plans Specialist, CRPS. He holds series 7, 63, 66 securities registrations with LPL Financial and a Group 1 Life and Variables Contract Insurance License.

Shane is a graduate of Texas Tech University (MSBA-Finance), Texas State University (BBA-Finance), and a CERTIFIED FINANCIAL PLANNER professional. He holds series 7, 24, 53, 63 and 66 securities registrations with LPL Financial and a Group 1 Life and Variable Contract Insurance License.

They speak to audiences across the country, speaking to both sudden wealth recipients and the advisors, agents, and reps that represent them. Quartz Financial is based in Austin, Texas.

www.SuddenWealthCenter.com

Content provided in this material is for general information only and not intended to provide

About the Authors

specific advice or recommendations for any individual. At time of publication, securities and advisory services are offered through LPL Financial, a registered investment advisor, Member FINRA and SIPC.